21世纪高等院校财经管理系列实用规划教材·国际贸易系列

国际经贸英语阅读教程

主编 李晓娣 梁河

北京大学出版社
PEKING UNIVERSITY PRESS

内 容 简 介

本书精选了原版英美专业教材、论文与报刊时文，语言地道、规范，知识性强，并体现国际经济与贸易发展的前沿与热点。

本书共分为国际贸易理论与政策、国际贸易实务、国际金融、国际合作与跨国公司、国际营销与管理5个单元；除了对经典国际贸易理论及政策进行系统讲解外，还对国际贸易合同、运输与保险、货款收付、争端解决、国际收支、外汇与期权的相关知识给予了全面介绍，并涉及了国际营销与跨国公司管理领域的重点与热点问题。

本书适用于经济与管理类专业和相关专业的学生、对外经贸工作人员以及感兴趣的自学人员。

图书在版编目(CIP)数据

国际经贸英语阅读教程/李晓娣，梁河主编. —北京：北京大学出版社，2014.3
(21世纪高等院校财经管理系列实用规划教材·国际贸易系列)
ISBN 978-7-301-23876-9

Ⅰ.①国… Ⅱ.①李… ②梁… Ⅲ.①国际贸易—英语—阅读教学—高等学校—教材 Ⅳ.①H319.4

中国版本图书馆 CIP 数据核字(2014)第 020544 号

书　　　　名：	国际经贸英语阅读教程
著作责任者：	李晓娣　梁　河　主编
策 划 编 辑：	王显超　李　虎
责 任 编 辑：	王显超
标 准 书 号：	ISBN 978-7-301-23876-9/F·3855
出 版 发 行：	北京大学出版社
地　　　　址：	北京市海淀区成府路 205 号　100871
网　　　　址：	http://www.pup.cn　新浪官方微博：@北京大学出版社
电 子 邮 箱：	编辑部 pup6@pup.cn　总编室 zpup@pup.cn
电　　　　话：	邮购部 010-62752015　发行部 010-62750672　编辑部 010-62750667
印 　刷 　者：	北京虎彩文化传播有限公司
经 　销 　者：	新华书店
	787 毫米×960 毫米　16 开本　11 印张　158 千字
	2014 年 3 月第 1 版　2024 年 8 月第 7 次印刷
定　　　　价：	35.00 元

未经许可，不得以任何方式复制或抄袭本书之部分或全部内容。
版权所有，侵权必究
举报电话：010-62752024　电子邮箱：fd@pup.cn

前　言

本书精选了原版英美专业教材、论文与报刊时文，语言地道、规范，知识性强，力争体现国际经济与贸易发展的前沿与热点，旨在为国际经济与贸易专业的学生和从事经贸与管理行业的人员提供指导与参考。

本书共分为国际贸易理论与政策、国际贸易实务、国际金融、国际合作与跨国公司、国际营销与管理 5 个单元；除了对经典国际贸易理论及政策进行系统讲解外，还对国际贸易合同、运输与保险、货款收付、争端解决、国际收支、外汇与期权的相关知识给予了全面介绍，并涉及了国际营销与跨国公司管理领域的重点与热点问题。

本书根据教师多年的国际经贸英语授课经验，在将教师角色设定为学生学习专业英语的指导者和促进者的基础上，按照启发式与激发式教学的需要进行编写。书中各单元均设有精读、泛读、补充阅读、课文注释、词汇及扩展以及网络学习资料六部分内容，符合学生的学习规律与习惯，具有较强的可拓展性和引导性。

本书由来自哈尔滨工程大学的教师编写。教材的框架和提纲经集体讨论拟定。全书由哈尔滨工程大学李晓娣、梁河担任主编并进行统稿审定。在编写的过程中，编者力争使本教材体现出国际经济与贸易发展的前沿与热点，旨在为从事经济与贸易专业的人员提供指导与参考。本书适用于经济与管理类专业和相关专业的学生、对外经贸工作人员以及感兴趣的自学人员。

本书在写作过程中，参阅和引用了国内外的文献和著作，在此表示感谢！

由于编者水平有限，书中疏漏之处在所难免，希望读者批评指正。

编　者

2014 年 1 月

于哈尔滨

目 录

Unit 1 International Trade Theories and Policies 国际贸易理论与政策 1

Part 1 Intensive Reading 精读 1
- Passage 1 Comparative Advantage and International Trade 比较优势与国际贸易 1
- Passage 2 The Product Life Cycle Theory and International Trade 产品生命周期理论与国际贸易 2

Part 2 Extensive Reading 泛读 3
- Passage 1 An Overview of WTO 世界贸易组织概述 3
- Passage 2 Tariff Barriers 关税壁垒 7
- Passage 3 Non-tariff Barriers 非关税壁垒 12

Part 3 Academic Reading 学术阅读 17
- Passage Theory of Services Trade 服务贸易理论 17

Part 4 Reading Comprehension 阅读理解 24
- Passage 1 The Factor Proportions Theory 要素禀赋论 24
- Passage 2 Intra-industry Trade 产业内贸易理论 25

Part 5 课文注释 27
Part 6 词汇及扩展 27
Part 7 网络学习资源 28

Unit 2 International Trade Practices 国际贸易实务 30

Part 1 Intensive Reading 精读 30
- Passage 1 The Export Sales Contract 出口销售合同 30
- Passage 2 Shipping, Insurance and Customs 海运保险和海关 31
- Passage 3 Settling of Trade Disputes 国际贸易争端的解决 33

Part 2 Extensive Reading 泛读 34
- Passage 1 A Sample of Sales Contract 出口合同样本 34
- Passage 2 Issues Affecting International Contracts 影响国际商务合同的种种问题 36
- Passage 3 Trade Facilitation and Promotion 贸易便捷化与贸易促进 37

Part 3 Academic Reading 学术阅读 43
- Passage Measures of Trade Restrictiveness 贸易限制的测量 43

Part 4 Reading Comprehension 阅读理解 48

		Passage 1	Clinton Is Right 克林顿没错	48
		Passage 2	International Trade and Economic Development 国际贸易与经济发展	50
	Part 5	课文注释		52
	Part 6	词汇及扩展		55
	Part 7	网络学习资源		56

Unit 3 International Finance 国际金融 ... 57

	Part 1	Intensive Reading 精读		57
		Passage 1	The International Monetary Fund 国际货币基金组织	57
		Passage 2	The International Reserve 国际储备	58
		Passage 3	What Are Futures Markets 什么是期货市场	59
		Passage 4	Hedging: How It Works 套期保值如何运作	59
		Passage 5	What Is a Stock 什么是股票	60
	Part 2	Extensive Reading 泛读		60
		Passage 1	Balance of Payments 国际收支	60
		Passage 2	Foreign Exchange Market 国际外汇市场	66
		Passage 3	The World Bank 世界银行	70
		Passage 4	Stock Prices 股票价格	71
	Part 3	Academic Reading 学术阅读		72
		Passage	Global Financial Stability Still at Risk 全球金融稳定依然面临风险	72
	Part 4	Reading Comprehension 阅读理解		83
		Passage 1	International Financial Market 国际金融市场	83
		Passage 2	A Strong Stock Market 强大的股票市场	85
		Passage 3	The Falling U.S. Dollar 贬值的美元	86
	Part 5	课文注释		88
	Part 6	词汇及扩展		93
	Part 7	网络学习资源		95

Unit 4 International Cooperation and Transnational Corporation 国际合作与跨国公司 ... 96

	Part 1	Intensive Reading 精读		96
		Passage 1	The Joint International Venture 国际合资企业	96
		Passage 2	International Technological Transfer 国际技术转让	98
		Passage 3	Transnational Corporations 跨国公司	100

目　录

　　Part 2　Extensive Reading　泛读 102
　　　Passage 1　Economic Policy of Open Economy 开放的经济政策 102
　　　Passage 2　Open China Economy 开放的中国经济 107
　　Part 3　Academic Reading　学术阅读 111
　　　Passage　Host Country Resource Availability and Resource Dependence Theory
　　　　　母国资源的可获得性与资源依赖理论 111
　　Part 4　Reading Comprehension　阅读理解 123
　　　Passage 1　A Smuggling Syndicate 走私辛迪加 123
　　　Passage 2　FDI and Business Acquisitions 直接投资与并购 124
　　Part 5　课文注释 126
　　Part 6　词汇及扩展 128
　　Part 7　网络学习资源 130

Unit 5　International Marketing and Management 国际营销与管理 131

　　Part 1　Intensive Reading　精读 131
　　　Passage 1　International Marketing 国际市场营销 131
　　　Passage 2　International Marketing Communications 综合营销沟通 ... 133
　　　Passage 3　Public Relations and the Net 公共关系和网络 135
　　Part 2　Extensive Reading　泛读 137
　　　Passage 1　International Marketing Planning and Strategy 国际营销计划与策略 137
　　　Passage 2　E-commercial 电子商务 139
　　Part 3　Academic Reading　学术阅读 143
　　　Passage　SWOT Analysis SWOT 分析法 143
　　Part 4　Reading Comprehension　阅读理解 157
　　　Passage 1　The Intuition of Senior Management 高级管理者的直觉 ... 157
　　　Passage 2　Advertisement 广告 159
　　Part 5　课文注释 161
　　Part 6　词汇及扩展 164
　　Part 7　网络学习资源 166

阅读理解部分参考答案 167

参考文献 168

Unit 1 International Trade Theories and Policies
国际贸易理论与政策

Part 1 Intensive Reading 精读

Passage 1 Comparative Advantage and International Trade 比较优势与国际贸易

It seems that most countries of the world have a strong desire to mutually expand their trade. At first sight, different nations appear to have many different economic, political and social reasons for wanting to trade. Under the surface, however, there is a common financial advantage enabling all countries to make a profit through international trade.

In his original state, man was self-sufficient, providing food, shelter and clothing, simple though it was, for his family. *It did not take long, however, for him to realize that there were some things he was more capable of doing than others and that it would benefit him to concentrate his efforts on the production of those goods in which he was particularly proficient and leave others to produce the goods that called for skills which he did not possess. This was the beginning of specialization.* And specialization on an international basis has now proved to be really worthwhile.

The concepts of absolute and comparative advantage play a crucial role in the specialization between countries. A country has an absolute advantage in the marketing of a product if it is the sole producer, or can produce it for less than anyone else. Examples of absolute advantage are rare since few nations are sole producers and economic conditions rapidly alter production costs.

A more realistic approach toward international specialization is that of comparative advantage. This concept says that a nation has a comparative advantage in an item if it can produce it more efficiently than alternative products. *Nations will usually produce and export those goods in which they have the greatest comparative advantage, and import those items in which they have the least comparative advantage.* For example, the United States, being a highly industrialized nation with good natural resources, tends to export manufactured items and natural resources, such as coal. By contrast, countries with low-cost labor tend to specialized in products that require a significant labor content such as textiles, shoes, and clothing.

Passage 2 The Product Life Cycle Theory and International Trade
产品生命周期理论与国际贸易

The product life cycle is based upon the biological life cycle. For example, a seed is planted (introduction); it begins to sprout (growth), it shoots out leaves and puts down roots as it becomes an adult (maturity); after a long period as an adult the plant begins to shrink and die out (decline).

In theory, it's the same for a product. Individual products pass through distinct phases: after a period of research and development, and trial manufacture, there is a period of introduction characterized by slow growth and high development cost. This is followed by a period of growth as sales and profits rise. A phase of maturity and saturation is then experienced as sales level off and the first signs of decline occur. The final phase is decline, characterized by lower sales and reduced profits, and eventually withdrawal, even final disappearance from the market.

However, in reality very few products follow such a prescriptive cycle. The length of each stage varies enormously. The decisions of marketers can change the stage, for example, from maturity to decline by price cutting. Not all products go through each stage. Some go from introduction directly to decline. It is not easy for us to tell which stage the product is in.

Product life-cycle theory suggests that long-term patterns of international trade are influenced by product innovation and subsequent diffusion. A country that produces technically superior goods will sell these goods first to its domestic market, then to other technically advanced countries. Developing countries will initially import and later manufacture these goods, by which stage the original innovator will have produced new products with more advanced technology.

This usually applies to explain international trade of the technology-intensive product. Because of the technological advantage it has, the innovating country is the sole producing and exporting country of the new product in the stage of production. After some time, several other technically advanced countries learn the new technology and begun to produce and export the product. Meanwhile, the developing countries which have no technological advantage import the new product from the innovating country and the several other technically advanced countries. This situation will continue to the stage of growth. When it comes to the stage of maturity, some developing countries may also learn the technology and begin to produce even export the product while the innovator has begun to reduce the production and upgrade the technology. Finally, in the stage of decline, the innovator and then the other technically advanced countries, may stop the production of the "old" product and import it from the developing countries. Meanwhile, the innovator has begun the stage of introduction of another new technological product.

Many cases could be found in reality to attest the theory. For example, many electronic home appliances, such as TVs, washing machine, micro-wave oven, were innovated in U.S., the firstly technologically advanced country in the present world. But now it is very difficult to find the domestic manufactures of these products in U.S. and almost all these appliances used in the families in U.S. are now imported from the developing countries including China.

Part 2 Extensive Reading 泛读

Passage 1 An Overview of WTO 世界贸易组织概述

The World Trade Organization (WTO) deals with the rules of trade between nations at a global or near-global level. But there is more to it than that.

Essentially, the WTO is a place where member governments go, to try to sort out the trade problems they face with each other. The first step is to talk. The WTO was born out of negotiations, and everything the WTO does is the result of negotiations. The bulk of the WTO's current work comes from the 1986-94 negotiations called the Uruguay Round and earlier negotiations under the General Agreement on Tariffs and Trade (GATT). The WTO is currently the host to new negotiations, under the "Doha Development Agenda" launched in 2001.

Where countries have faced trade barriers and wanted them lowered, the negotiations have helped to liberalize trade. But the WTO is not just about liberalizing trade, and in some circumstances its rules support maintaining trade barriers — for example to protect consumers and prevent the spread of disease.

1. Function

At its heart are the WTO agreements, negotiated and signed by the bulk of the world's trading nations. These documents provide the legal ground-rules for international commerce. They are essentially contracts, binding governments to keep their trade policies within agreed limits. Although negotiated and signed by governments, the goal is to help producers of goods and services, exporters, and importers conduct their business, while allowing governments to meet social and environmental objectives.

The system's overriding purpose is to help trade flow as freely as possible — so long as there are no undesirable side-effects. That partly means removing obstacles. It also means ensuring that individuals, companies and governments know what the trade rules are around the world, and giving them the confidence that there will be no sudden changes of policy. In other words, the rules have to be "transparent" and predictable.

This is a third important side to the WTO's work. Trade relations often involve conflicting interests. Agreements, including those painstakingly negotiated in the WTO system, often need interpreting. The most harmonious way to settle these differences is through some neutral procedure based on an agreed legal foundation. That is the purpose behind the dispute settlement process written into the WTO agreements.

2. Basic Principles

The WTO agreements are lengthy and complex because they are legal texts covering a wide range of activities. They deal with agriculture, textiles and clothing, banking, telecommunications, government purchases, industrial standards and product safety, food sanitation regulations, intellectual property, and much more. But a number of simple, fundamental principles run throughout all of these documents. These principles are the foundation of the multilateral trading system.

(1) Trade without Discrimination

① Most-favored-nation (MFN): treating other people equally.

Under the WTO agreements, countries cannot normally discriminate between their trading partners. Grant someone a special favor (such as a lower customs duty rate for one of their products) and you have to do the same for all other WTO members.

This principle is known as most-favored-nation (MFN) treatment (see box). It is so important that it is the first article of the General Agreement on Tariffs and Trade (GATT), which governs trade in goods. MFN is also a priority in the General Agreement on Trade in Services (GATS) (Article 2) and the Agreement on Trade-Related Aspects of Intellectual Property Rights (TRIPS) (Article 4), although in each agreement the principle is handled slightly differently. Together, those three agreements cover all three main areas of trade handled by the WTO.

Some exceptions are allowed. For example, countries can set up a free trade agreement that applies only to goods traded within the group — discriminating against goods from outside. Or they can give developing countries special access to their markets. Or a country can raise barriers against products that are considered to be traded unfairly from specific countries. And in services, countries are allowed, in limited circumstances, to discriminate. But the agreements only permit these exceptions under strict conditions. In general, MFN means that every time a country lowers a trade barrier or opens up a market, it has to do so for the same goods or services from all its trading partners — whether rich or poor, weak or strong.

② National treatment: treating foreigners and locals equally.

Imported and locally-produced goods should be treated equally — at least after the foreign goods have entered the market. The same should apply to foreign and domestic services, and to foreign and local trademarks, copyrights and patents. This principle of "national treatment" (giving others the same treatment as one's own nationals) is also found in all the three main WTO agreements (Article 3 of GATT, Article 17 of GATS and Article 3 of TRIPS), although once again the principle is handled slightly differently in each of these.

National treatment only applies once a product, service or item of intellectual property has entered the market. Therefore, charging customs duty on an import is not a violation of national treatment even if locally-produced products are not charged an equivalent tax.

(2) Free Trade: Gradually, through Negotiation

Lowering trade barriers is one of the most obvious means of encouraging trade. The barriers concerned include customs duties (or tariffs) and measures such as import bans or quotas that restrict quantities selectively. From time to time other issues such as red tape and exchange rate policies have also been discussed. Since GATT's creation in 1947-48 there have been eight rounds of trade negotiations. A ninth round, under the Doha Development Agenda, is now underway. At first these focused on lowering tariffs (customs duties) on imported goods. As a result of the negotiations, by the mid-1990s industrial countries' tariff rates on industrial goods had fallen steadily to less than 4%.

But by the 1980s, the negotiations had expanded to cover non-tariff barriers on goods, and to the new areas such as services and intellectual property.

Opening markets can be beneficial, but it also requires adjustment. The WTO agreements allow countries to introduce changes gradually, through "progressive liberalization". Developing countries are usually given longer to fulfill their obligations.

(3) Predictability: through Binding and Transparency

Sometimes, promising not to raise a trade barrier can be as important as lowering one, because the promise gives businesses a clearer view of their future opportunities. With stability and predictability, investment is encouraged, jobs are created and consumers can fully enjoy the benefits of competition — choice and lower prices. The multilateral trading system is an attempt by governments to make the business environment stable and predictable.

In the WTO, when countries agree to open their markets for goods or services, they "bind" their commitments. For goods, these bindings amount to ceilings on customs tariff rates. Sometimes countries tax imports at rates that are lower than the bound rates. Frequently this is the case in developing countries. In developed countries the rates actually charged and the bound rates tend to be the same. A country can change its bindings, but only after negotiating with its trading partners, which could mean compensating them for loss of trade. One of the achievements of the Uruguay Round of multilateral trade talks was to increase the amount of trade under binding commitments (see table). In agriculture, 100% of products now have bound tariffs. The result of all this: a substantially higher degree of market security for traders and investors.

The system tries to improve predictability and stability in other ways as well. One way is to discourage the use of quotas and other measures used to set limits on quantities of imports — administering quotas can lead to more red-tape and accusations of unfair play. Another is to make countries' trade rules as clear and public ("transparent") as possible. Many WTO agreements require governments to disclose their policies and practices publicly within the country or by notifying the WTO. The regular surveillance of national trade policies through the Trade Policy Review Mechanism provides a further means of encouraging transparency both domestically and at the multilateral level.

(4) Promoting Fair Competition

The WTO is sometimes described as a "free trade" institution, but that is not entirely accurate. The system does allow tariffs and, in limited circumstances, other forms of protection. More accurately, it is a system of rules dedicated to open, fair and undistorted competition.

The rules on non-discrimination — MFN and national treatment — are designed to secure fair conditions of trade. So are those on dumping (exporting at below cost to gain market share) and subsidies. The issues are complex, and the rules try to establish what is fair or unfair, and how governments can respond, in particular by charging additional import duties calculated to compensate for damage caused by unfair trade. Many of the other WTO agreements aim to support fair competition: in agriculture, intellectual property, services, for example. The agreement on government procurement (a "plurilateral" agreement because it is signed by only a few WTO members) extends competition rules to purchases by thousands of government entities in many countries. And so on.

(5) Encouraging Development and Economic Reform

The WTO system contributes to development. On the other hand, developing countries need flexibility in the time they take to implement the system's agreements. And the agreements themselves inherit the earlier provisions of GATT that allow for special assistance and trade concessions for developing countries.

Over three quarters of WTO members are developing countries and countries in transition to market economies. During the seven and a half years of the Uruguay Round, over 60 of these countries implemented trade liberalization programmes autonomously. At the same time, developing countries and transition economies were much more active and influential in the Uruguay Round negotiations than in any previous round, and they are even more so in the current Doha Development Agenda.

International Trade Theories and Policies 国际贸易理论与政策

At the end of the Uruguay Round, developing countries were prepared to take on most of the obligations that are required of developed countries. But the agreements did give them transition periods to adjust to the more unfamiliar and difficult WTO provisions — particularly so for the poorest, "least-developed" countries. A ministerial decision adopted at the end of the round says better-off countries should accelerate implementing market access commitments on goods exported by the least-developed countries, and it seeks increased technical assistance for them. More recently, developed countries have started to allow duty-free and quota-free imports for almost all products from least-developed countries. On all of this, the WTO and its members are still going through a learning process. The current Doha Development Agenda includes developing countries' concerns about the difficulties they face in implementing the Uruguay Round agreements.

Passage 2 Tariff Barriers 关税壁垒

The tariff barriers, and the non-tariff barriers, of the importing country, may hamper accessibility to an import market. The tariff barriers or import restraints are to protect the domestic manufacturers or producers from foreign competition. Export products generally become less competitive, or uncompetitive, as a result of the barriers.

1. The Tariff Concept

A tariff is simply a tax (duty) levied on a product when it crosses national boundaries. The most widespread tariff is the *import tariff*, which is a tax levied on an imported product. A less common tariff is an *export tariff*, which is a tax imposed on an exported product. Export tariffs have often been used by developing nations. For example, cocoa exports have been taxed by Ghana, and oil exports have been taxed by the Organization of Petroleum Exporting Countries (OPEC) in order to raise revenue or promote scarcity in global markets and hence increase the world price.

Did you know that the United States cannot levy export tariffs? When the U.S. Constitution was written, southern cotton-producing states feared that northern textile-manufacturing states would pressure the federal government into levying export tariffs to depress the price of cotton. An export duty would lead to decreased exports and thus a fall in the price of cotton within the United States. As the result of negotiations, the Constitution was worded so as to prevent export taxes: "No tax or duty shall be laid on articles exported from any state."

Tariffs may be imposed for protection or revenue purposes. A protective tariff is designed to insulate import-competing producers from foreign competition. Although a protective tariff generally is not intended to totally prohibit imports from entering the country, it does place foreign producers at a competitive disadvantage when selling in the domestic market. A revenue tariff is imposed for the purpose of generating tax revenues and may be placed on either exports or imports.

2. The Tariff Welfare Effects: Small-nation Model

To measure the effects of a tariff on a nation's welfare, consider the case of a nation whose imports constitute a very small portion of the world market supply. This small nation would be a *price taker,* facing a constant world price level for its import commodity. This is not a rare case; many nations are not important enough to influence the terms at which they trade.

In Figure 1.1, the small nation before trade produces at market equilibrium point *E*, as determined by the intersection of its domestic supply and demand schedules. At equilibrium price $9,500, the quantity supplied is 50 units, and the quantity demanded is 50 units. Now suppose that the economy is opened to foreign trade and that the world auto price is $8,000, less than the domestic price. Because the world market will supply an unlimited number of autos at price $8,000, the world supply schedule would appear as a horizontal (perfectly elastic) line. Line S_{d+w} shows the supply of autos available to the small-nation consumers from domestic and foreign sources combined. This overall supply schedule is the one that would prevail in free trade.

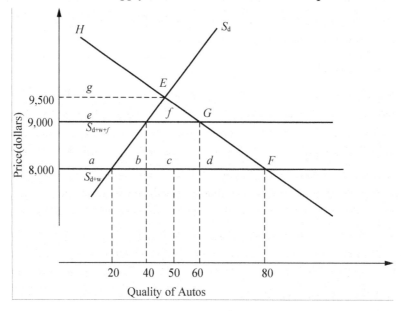

Figure 1.1   Tariff Trade and Welfare Effects: Small-nation Model

Under free trade, the domestic auto industry is being damaged by foreign competition. Industry sales and revenues are falling, and workers are losing their jobs. Suppose management and labor unite and convince the government to levy a protective tariff on auto imports. Assume the small nation imposes a tariff of $1,000 on auto imports. Because this small nation is not

International Trade Theories and Policies 国际贸易理论与政策　　Unit 1

important enough to influence world market conditions, the supply price of autos remains constant, unaffected by the tariff. This means that the small nation's terms of trade remains unchanged. The introduction of the tariff raises the home price of auto by the full amount of the duty, and the increase price falls entirely on the domestic consumer. The overall supply shifts upward by the amount of the tarriff, from S_{d+w} to S_{d+w+f}.

The protective tariff results in a new equilibrium quantity at point G, where the domestic auto price is $9,000. Domestic production increases by 20 units, whereas domestic consumption falls by 20 units. Imports decrease from their pretariff level of 60 units to 20 units. This reduction can be attributed to falling domestic consumption and rising domestic production. The effects of the tariff are to impede imports and protect domestic producers. But what are the tariff's effects on the national welfare? Figure 1.1 shows that before the tariff was levied, consumer surplus equaled areas $a + b + c + d + e + f + g$. With the tariff, consumer surplus falls to areas $e + f + g$, an overall loss in consumer surplus equal to areas $a + b + c + d$. This change affects the nation's welfare in a number of ways. The welfare effects of a tariff include a revenue effect, a redistribution effect, a protective effect, and a consumption effect. As might be expected, the tariff provides the government with additional tax revenue and benefits domestic auto producers; at the same time, however, it wastes resources and harms the domestic consumer.

The tariff's revenue effect represents the government's collections of duty. Found by multiplying the number of imports (20 units) times the tariff ($1,000), government revenue equals area c, or $20,000. This represents the portion of the loss of consumer surplus, in monetary terms, that is transferred to the government. For the nation as a whole, the revenue effect does not result in an overall welfare loss; consumer surplus is merely shifted from the private to the public sector.

The redistributive effect is the transfer of consumer surplus, in monetary terms, to the domestic producers of the import-competing product. This is represented by area a, which equals $30,000. Under the tariff, domestic home consumers will buy from domestic firms 40 autos at a price of $9,000, for a total expenditure of $360,000. At the free-trade price of $8,000, the same 40 autos would have yielded $320,000. The imposition of the tariff thus results in home producers' receiving additional revenues totaling areas $a + b$, or $40,000 (the difference between $360,000 and $320,000). As the tariff encourages domestic production to rise from 20 to 40 units, however, producers must pay part of the increased revenue as higher costs of producing the increased output, depicted by area b, or $10,000. The remaining revenue, $30,000, area a, is a net gain in producer income. The redistributive effect, therefore, is a transfer of income from consumers to producers. Like the revenue effect, it does not result in an overall loss of welfare for the economy. Area b, totaling $10,000, is referred to as the protective effect of the tariff. It illustrates the loss to the domestic economy resulting from wasted resources used to produce additional autos at increasing unit costs. As the tariff-induced domestic output expands, resources that are less adaptable to auto production are eventually used, increasing unit production costs. This means that resources are used less efficiently than they would have been with free trade, in which case autos would have been purchased from low-cost foreign producers. A tariff's protective effect thus arises because less efficient domestic production is substituted for more efficient foreign production. Referring to Figure 1.1, as domestic output increases from 20 to 40 units, the domestic cost of producing autos rises, as shown by supply schedule S_d. But the same increase in autos could have been obtained at a unit cost of $8,000 before the tariff was levied. Area *b,* which depicts the protective effect, represents a loss to the economy.

Most of the consumer surplus lost because of the tariff has been accounted for: *c* went to the government as revenue; *a* was transferred to home suppliers as income; and *b* was lost by the economy because of inefficient domestic production. The consumption effect, represented by area d , which equals $10,000, is the residual not accounted for elsewhere. It arises from the decrease in consumption resulting from the tariff's artificially increasing the price of autos from $8,000 to $9,000. A loss of welfare occurs because of the increased price and lower consumption. Like the protective effect, the consumption effect represents a real cost to society, not a transfer to other sectors of the economy. Together, these two effects equal the deadweight loss of the tariff (areas *b* + *d* in the Figure 1.1).

As long as it is assumed that a nation accounts for a negligible portion of international trade, its levying an import tariff necessarily lowers its national welfare. This is because there is no favorable welfare effect resulting from the tariff that would offset the deadweight loss of consumer surplus. If a nation could impose a tariff that would improve its terms of trade vis-à-vis its trading partners, it would enjoy a larger share of the gains from trade. This would tend to increase its national welfare, offsetting the deadweight loss of consumer surplus. Because it is so insignificant relative to the world market, however, a small nation is unable to influence the terms of trade. Levying an import tariff, therefore, reduces a small nation's welfare.

3. Import /Export Tariff

An import tariff is a tax collected on imported goods. Generally speaking, a tariff is any tax or fee collected by a government. Sometimes tariff is used in a non-trade context, as in railroad tariffs. However, the term is much more commonly applied to a tax on imported goods.

(1) Customs Duty Assessments

Customs duties are generally assessed in three ways: ad valorem duty, specific duty and compound duty.

Unit 1
International Trade Theories and Policies 国际贸易理论与政策

① A specific tariff.

A specific tariff is levied as a fixed charge per unit of imports. For example, the U.S. government levies a 5.1 cent specific tariff on every wristwatch imported into the U.S. Thus, if 1,000 watches are imported, the U.S. government collects $51 in tariff revenue. In this case, $51 is collected whether the watch is a $40 Swatch or a $5,000 Rolex.

② Ad valorem tariff.

An ad valorem tariff is levied as a fixed percentage of the value of the commodity imported. "Ad valorem" is Latin for "on value" or "in proportion to the value". The U.S. currently levies a 2.5% ad valorem tariff on imported automobiles. Thus if $100,000 worth of autos are imported, the US government collects $2,500 in tariff revenue. In this case, $2,500 is collected whether two $50,000 BMWs are imported or ten $10,000 Hyundais.

③ Compound duty.

Compound duty is assessed as a combination of the specific duty and ad valorem duty ($20 per kilogram net, plus 30% of FOB price).

Occasionally both a specific and an ad valorem tariff are levied on the same product simultaneously. This is known as a two-part tariff. For example, wristwatches imported into the U.S. face the 5.1 cent specific tariff as well as a 6.25% ad valorem tariff on the case and the strap and a 5.3% ad valorem tariff on the battery. Perhaps this should be called a three-part tariff!

As the above examples suggest, different tariffs are generally applied to different commodities. Governments rarely apply the same tariff to all goods and services imported into the country. One exception to this occurred in 1971 when President Nixon, in a last-ditch effort to save the Bretton-Woods system of fixed exchange rates, imposed a 10% ad valorem tariff on all imported goods from IMF member countries. But, incidents such as this are uncommon.

(2) High Customs Duty

The high import duties in many countries have been reduced under the former GATT (General Agreement on Tariffs and Trade) multilateral agreements. The GATT was formed in Geneva, Switzerland, in 1947 and it was succeeded by the WTO (World Trade Organization) on January 1, 1995. The organization, through multilateral agreements, helps reduce trade barriers between the signatory countries and promotes trade through tariff concessions. WTO has wide power to regulate international competition.

(3) Countervailing Duty

Countervailing duty is a duty imposed in addition to the regular (general) import duty, in order to counteract or offset the subsidy and bounty paid to foreign export-manufacturers by their government as an incentive to export, that would reduce the cost of goods. Imposing a countervailing duty is the answer to unfair competition from subsidized foreign goods.

(4) Anti-dumping Duty

Anti-dumping duty is a duty imposed to offset the advantage gained by the foreign exporters when they sell their goods to an importing country at a price far lower than their domestic selling price or below cost. Dumping usually occurs from the oversupply of goods, which is often a result of overproduction, and from disposing of obsolete goods to other markets.

Passage 3　Non-tariff Barriers 非关税壁垒

Non-tariff barriers are government laws, regulations, policies, conditions, restrictions, or specific requirements, and private sector business practices or prohibitions, which protect the domestic industries from foreign competition. They are the means of keeping the foreign goods out of domestic market while abiding by the multilateral agreements that the country has signed through the WTO (World Trade Organization).

1. Quotas

(1) Import Quotas

Import quotas are limitations on the quantity of goods that can be imported into the country during a specified period of time. An import quota is typically set below the free trade level of imports. In this case it is called a binding quota. If a quota is set at or above the free trade level of imports then it is referred to as a non-binding quota. Goods that are illegal within a country effectively have a quota set equal to zero. Thus many countries have a zero quota on narcotics and other illicit drugs.

There are two basic types of quotas: absolute quotas and tariff-rate quotas. Absolute quotas limit the quantity of imports to a specified level during a specified period of time. Sometimes these quotas are set globally and thus affect all imports while sometimes they are set only against specified countries. Absolute quotas are generally administered on a first-come first-served basis. For this reason, many quotas are filled shortly after the opening of the quota period. Tariff-rate quotas allow a specified quantity of goods to be imported at a reduced tariff rate during the specified quota period.

(2) Export Quota

Export quota is the number or amount of goods of a specific kind or class that the government of exporting country will allow to be exported. The purpose of export quota is to protect the domestic supply of the goods, for example, sugar, cement and lumber. Export quota

International Trade Theories and Policies 国际贸易理论与政策

may also be used to boost the world prices of such commodities as oil and strategic metals, and to protect the natural resources of the exporting country.

The term quota usually refers to the import quota. In practice, the term export quota often, but incorrectly, refers to the import quota. When exporters talk about the export quota, most often they are referring to the import quota of the importing country. The quota is allocated, in the form of a permit or a license, to the exporters (the export-manufacturers and export-traders) usually on pro rata, based on their past export records. The quota allocation normally is administered by the government export office or the national industry association of the exporting country, for example garment manufacturers' association and footwear manufacturers' association.

For new exporters, the chance of being given a quota by the administering office is often slim. However, they can still export either by selling their products to exporters with excess quota—having a quota but for reasons like shortage of supply, they are unable to serve or utilize all the amount or quantity allocated by the administering office—or by "buying" the excess quota from willing sellers (exporters), with approval from the administering office. To ensure that the quota granted to an exporting country is fully served or utilized within a given time, the administering office of that country may allow the "quota buying" between exporters. When a quota is reached, imports from an exporting country cannot be legally obtained. Hence, the quota is more effective in limiting imports than the tariff barriers.

2. Voluntary Import Expansions (VIEs)

A Voluntary Import Expansion (VIE) is an agreement to increase the quantity of imports of a product over a specified period of time. In the late 1980s, VIEs were suggested by the U.S. as a way of expanding U.S. exports into Japanese markets. Under the assumption that Japan maintained barriers to trade that restricted the entry of U.S. exports, Japan was asked to increase its volume of imports on specified products including semiconductors, automobiles, auto parts, medical equipment and flat glass. The intention was that VIEs would force a pattern of trade that more closely replicated the free trade level.

3. Export Subsidies

Export subsidies are payments made by the government to encourage the export of specified products. As with taxes, subsidies can be levied on a specific or ad valorem basis. The most common product groups where export subsidies are applied are agricultural and dairy products.

Most countries have income support programs for their nation's farmers. These are often motivated by national security or self-sufficiency considerations. Farmers' incomes are maintained by restricting domestic supply, raising domestic demand, or a combination of the two.

One common method is the imposition of price floors on specified commodities. When there is excess supply at the floor price, however, the government must stand ready to purchase the excess. These purchases are often stored for future distribution when there is a shortfall of supply at the floor price. Sometimes the amount the government must purchase exceeds the available storage capacity. In this case, the government must either build more storage facilities, at some cost, or devise an alternative method to dispose of the surplus inventory. It is in these situations, or to avoid these situations, that export subsidies are sometimes used. By encouraging exports, the government will reduce the domestic supply and eliminate the need for the government to purchase the excess.

One of the main export subsidy programs in the U.S. is called the Export Enhancement Program (EEP). Its stated purpose is to help U.S. farmers compete with farm products from other subsidizing countries, especially the European Union, in targeted countries. The EEP's major objectives are to challenge unfair trade practices, to expand U.S. agricultural exports, and to encourage other countries exporting agricultural commodities to undertake serious negotiations on agricultural trade problems. As a result of Uruguay Round commitments, the U.S. has established annual export subsidy quantity ceilings by commodity and maximum budgetary expenditures. Commodities eligible under EEP initiatives are wheat, wheat flour, semolina, rice, frozen poultry, frozen pork, barley, barley malt, table eggs, and vegetable oil.

In recent years the U.S. government has made annual outlays of over $1 billion in its agricultural Export Enhancement Program (EEP) and its Dairy Export Incentive Program (DEIP). The EU has spent over $4 billion annually to encourage exports of its agricultural and dairy products.

4. Counter-trade

Counter-trade is a generic term that describes various techniques for the conditional exchange of goods and/or services between seller and buyer. In layman's parlance, countertrade is "You buy from me and I will buy from you". As the trade reciprocation entails a requirement to buy in exchange for a right to sell, it is indeed a form of non-tariff barrier.

Counter-trade provides a means of trade with countries using a blocked currency—currency that is not readily convertible into other currencies—or lacking the foreign exchange, thus removing the difficulties and risks in a trade financing and paving the way for a successful deal that otherwise would fail. Counter-trade also provides a means to preserve foreign exchange reserves by eliminating the use of hard currency.

Counter-trade is thriving in modern international trade. In early 1970's, counter-trade was used by about 20 countries and now, more than 100 countries are using it. A wide range of goods and services are transacted on counter-trade, for example, oil, airplanes, automobiles, mineral, machinery, agricultural products, shoes, wine, and advertising time.

(1) Barter

Barter is the direct exchange of goods and/or services, of approximately equivalent value, between parties without the use of money or credit.

(2) Offset

Offset is found most often in the large-scale capital goods, such as commercial aircrafts and military hardware.

Offset is either direct or indirect. In a direct offset, part of the cost of the export product is offset by buying the agreed amount of goods—components or materials—from the importing country, which the exporter incorporates in the export product. Other direct offsets include coproduction, licensing, subcontracting, and joint ventures.

(3) Compensation or Buyback

Compensation or buyback is normally found in the exports of plants, machinery or technology, where the exporter is compensated by, or obliged to buy from the importer, the goods produced by such plants, machinery or technology.

(4) Counter-purchase or Parallel Barter

The seller is obliged to buy from the buyer goods and/or services that are usually unrelated to the goods and/or services sold by the seller. The counter-purchase involves two separate contracts and the deliveries can take place within a period of one to five years.

(5) Clearing Agreement

Two countries agree to buy particular types and quantities of each other's goods within a period of time, using a designated clearing currency. At the end of the period, the country that buys more may settle the shortfall either in hard currency and/or goods, or issue a credit to the other country in the subsequent clearing agreement, if any.

5. Import Levies

Levies on imported and transit goods are often collected from the use of ports and terminal facilities. They are collected to pay the costs of maintenance and development of the infrastructures. Levies may vary from port to port (or point to point) within a country.

6. Export Pre-shipment Inspection

The government normally requires some form of inspection for health, safety, security, and tax purposes, before goods are allowed to leave or enter a country. The government pre-shipment inspection on some export goods, such as electrical and electronic items, is required in many exporting countries in order to protect the country's quality image abroad and the foreign consumers.

7. Import Pre-shipment Inspection

Certain importing countries require—stipulate in the letter of credit—pre-shipment inspection by their government engaged independent surveyor, which is a form of non-tariff barrier. The import government may pay an annual fee to the official surveyor. Moreover, in practice, an inspection fee is collected from the exporter in each shipment.

The main purpose of the inspection, conducted at the exporting country, is price and quantity verification, in order to stamp out rampant import under-declaration where the government loses a lot on tax revenue. The inspection has increased the government import collection but not to the level expected, that is, the under-declaration continues. Importers would be discouraged to under-declare imports if the duty was low. Consequently, government may collect more duties and taxes and save additional inspection expenses.

The inspection was restricted to shipments coming from certain developing countries, but later included all countries. Exporters from developed countries who have been selling, without under-declaration, to the importing countries concerned for decades are affected, too. In reality, the export price is often lower than the domestic selling price. The surveyor's inspection tends to compare the export invoice price against the domestic selling price in the exporting country. The pre-shipment inspection generates dissent and discontent from exporters and importers.

8. Consular Invoice or Legalization or Visa of Export Documents

Certain importing countries, particularly in Central America, require a Consular Invoice. The consular fee can be a percentage of the invoice value. Some importing countries require that the export documents be legalized or visaed by their Consulate or the Commercial Section of the Embassy located in the exporting country. A fee is usually charged.

9. Health, Safety and Technical Standards

Certain products require the health certificate, safety test marks, or standards certification of the importing country before they are allowed entry. The product modification may be needed to meet the import requirements, which means additional product inventory and expenses. The U.S. generally has more regulations than other countries governing the use of some goods, such as pharmaceuticals. These regulations can have an effect upon trade patterns even though the policies are not designed based on their effects on trade.

10. Currency Deposit in Importations

Currency deposit, in local or foreign currency, may be required in applying for a letter of credit (L/C) and/or an import permit. In practice, many banks require a deposit and the amount

International Trade Theories and Policies 国际贸易理论与政策

varies from bank to bank. In times of foreign exchange shortage in a country, the government may require a 100% deposit in foreign currency (U.S. Dollar usually).

11. Product Labeling in Foreign Language

Product labeling in the official language of the importing country is often required, especially health and food products, which normally require the name of manufacturer and product expiry date. It may mean having new packaging to conform to import requirements. Consequently, additional product inventory and expenses are often necessary.

12. Closed Market Distribution

The closed market distribution can be a government and/or a private sector business practice or prohibition that precludes foreign goods from the domestic distribution channels. This may occur in a country having a centrally planned economy or a deep sense of nationalism.

13. Advertising Restrictions

In some countries, the comparative advertising—naming or showing of competing products—is prohibited by laws. The kind of product and the extend of advertising claims are regulated, which may render the advertisement less effective. Violators could face heavy penalties.

14. Government Procurement Policies

A Government Procurement Policy requires that a specified percentage of purchases by the federal or state governments be made from domestic firms rather than foreign firms.

15. Red-Tape Barriers

Red-tape barriers refers to costly administrative procedures required for the importation of foreign goods. Red-tape barriers can take many forms. France once required that videocassette recorders enter the country through one small port facility in the south of France. Because the port capacity was limited, it effectively restricted the number of VCRs that could enter the country. A red-tape barrier may arise if multiple licenses must be obtained from a variety of government sources before importation of a product is allowed.

Part 3   Academic Reading   学术阅读

Passage   Theory of Services Trade 服务贸易理论

What is different about trade in services compared with trade in goods? There are many points that could be emphasized. In this section, we provide a broad overview of the theory on the mechanics of international services trade and some of the implications this carries for public policy and the gains from trade. The emphasis on alternative modes through which international exchange may occur, market structure, and regulation also guides much of the empirical and political economy literature reviewed in the sections that follow.

1. The Proximity Burden

Because, by definition, services are a flow and so are not storable, their exchange frequently requires the proximity of supplier and consumer. Providers must move to the location of the buyer/consumer of a service, or vice versa (Hill 1977). Given the need for proximity in exchange, factors like distance place a cost burden on certain forms of services delivery. This is the proximity burden (Elisabeth Christen and Francois 2010).

Beginning in the early 1980s, technological change has progressively weakened the proximity burden. In an early paper on this phenomenon, Bhagwati (1984a) explored its implications, emphasizing mechanisms through which services are "disembodied" or "splintered" from goods or people as "carriers". He argued that trade in services may expand as a result of the incentive to "splinter" the production chain geographically, not just in terms of tangible inputs but also services. The more recent literature calls this process fragmentation. Fragmentation in turn may lead to basic changes in the structure and pattern of trade, as low-wage activities can be sliced away and outsourced. Of course, the fragmentation of production is not an issue unique to services trade (Francois 1990b; Ronald W. Jones and HenrykKierzkowski 1990; Richard Baldwin and Robert-Nicoud 2007). However, the significance of underlying proximity constraints for service transactions to be feasible means that "trade" may require a heavier dose of local presence of suppliers in the mix of cross-border and locally supplied services than is the case with goods. Indeed, while the standard definition of outsourcing is broad—including all inputs acquired from unaffiliated companies (Elhanan Helpman 2006)—the recent outsourcing literature focuses more narrowly on arms-length intermediate service transactions with foreign firms (Mary Amiti and Shang-Jin Wei 2005; Bhagwati, Panagariya, and T. N. Srinivasan 2004).

In general, services provision will often have an element of "jointness in production" in the sense that complementary inputs— including other services—are needed to allow effective exchange (trade) of a service to occur. This is recognized in the policy community, where the cross-border and local presence (or commercial establishment) components of international service transactions are referred to as modes of supply. Indeed, an important paper by Gary P. Sampson and Richard H. Snape (1985) developed the typology for modes that was largely incorporated in the design of the GATS. The first of these modes, what has come to be called mode 1 in GATS-speak, is cross-border supply. It applies when service suppliers resident in one country provide services in another country, without either supplier or buyer/consumer moving to the physical location of the other. Mode 2, consumption abroad, refers to a consumer resident in one country moving to the location of the supplier(s) to consume a service. Mode 3, commercial presence, refers to legal persons (firms) moving to the location of consumers to sell services locally through the establishment of a foreign affiliate or branch. The fourth mode of supply, mode 4 or movement of natural persons, refers to a process through which individuals (temporarily) move to the country of the consumer to provide the service. In reality, there are services where the proximity burden remains so strong that delivery must be local, so that foreign ownership (establishment) is required (mode 3). We summarize the four modes in Table 1-1.

Table 1-1 GATS-speak

Mode 1: direct cross-border trade in services
Mode 2: movement of the customer to the country of the provider
Mode 3: sales of services through an offshore affiliate (legal person)
Mode 4: (temporary) movement of (natural) persons to provide services

Jointness in production has a number of implications for the normative and positive aspects of trade and foreign investment in services. For example, jointness means there may be basic inconsistencies between potential trade flow rankings in services and relative domestic price rankings, complicating the analysis of potential trade volumes, as well as the estimation of trade barriers based on price comparisons, i.e., apparently higher priced markets may actually have comparative export advantage (Alan V. Deardorff 1985). In addition, asymmetric information and the resulting need for regulation also implies that regulatory regimes affecting the (temporary) movement of people and the longer-term establishment of service suppliers (e.g., visa restrictions and economic needs tests; FDI policies) are important determinants of the feasibility of trade in services. Finally, proximity requirements also lead to potential complementarity in modes of protection on trade and FDI. Cross-border trade restrictions may limit FDI incentives, while restrictions on the operations of foreign firms may limit cross-border trade in goods (Hindley 1988). We focus on this issue in the following subsection on modes of supply and the theory of the firm. It should be borne in mind that, in many cases, the proximity burden is complete in that sales can only be accomplished locally, with little or no scope for cross-border trade-movement of suppliers or consumers is required.

2. Modes of Supply and the Firm

The international mechanisms (the GATS and regional integration agreements) that discipline government policies affecting the foreign activities of service firms emphasize alternative channels for market access, and negotiations are structured around improved conditions for access through these channels. An important question therefore relates to how the combination of cross-border trade and establishment trade is realized. Does it take place within firms (a mix of intrafirm and establishment trade) or occur through armslength (unaffiliated) trade? Understanding this involves internalization incentives, the benefits of licensing service technologies, and the decision (and feasibility) of service firms to sell cross-border, invest locally, or engage in a mix of the two.

In a sense, the questions outlined in the paragraph above are very similar to those addressed in the literature on horizontal versus vertical FDI for goods-producing firms. In particular, the integrating approach called the "knowledge-capital model" of FDI, and recent theoretical work on the boundary of the firm and firm efficiency (Pol Antràs 2003; Bruce A. Blonigen, Ronald B. Davies, and Keith Head 2003; Wilfred J. Ethier and Markusen 1996; Markusen and Keith E. Maskus 2002; Markusen 2002; Helpman, Marc J. Melitz, and Stephen R. Yeaple 2004; Helpman 2006) focus on similar questions. There are, however, potentially important differences (Markusen and Bridget Strand 2009). The literature on foreign production by multinational enterprises (MNEs) in goods emphasizes trade-offs between coordination costs and trade costs (both physical transport costs and policy-driven costs) on the one hand, and potentially higher costs of foreign production linked to management of multiplant operations. For services, we do not have physical transport costs that hinge on distance, while conceptually FDI may involve local establishments that do not serve primarily as production nodes or plants, but rather as transit points for sale of home production to foreign markets. Furthermore, distance costs may be linked to problems of coordination when dealing with customers, rather than with problems linked to physical loading and shipping of goods. Indeed, recent evidence suggests that, at the aggregate level of industries and total flows, the collective response of individual service firms to distance leads to a striking difference in the impact of distance on the mix of establishment based sales and direct export sales when we compare goods and services (Christen and Francois 2010; Carolina Lennon 2008).

Another pattern in the data to be explained theoretically is variation in the mix between unaffiliated (external) trade in services, affiliated (internal) trade, and delivery through foreign establishments. While there is an exploratory literature on the empirical aspects of this relationship, the theoretical foundations remain weak. In our view, the new theory on firm selection and efficiency provides some insight here, and promises a useful framework for analysis of firm-level choice of modes in the service sector. Kristian Behrens and Gianmarco I. P. Ottaviano (forthcoming) provide a useful synthesis for our purposes, working with a stylized representation of recent firm models to explore a range of issues affecting goods producing firms. Given a mix of trade and coordination costs, there is a natural sorting into local, exporting, and MNEs driven by variations in firm productivity. Turning to the decision to internalize transactions, they examine good-producing firms that face the same physical trade costs for exports, while shipments outside the firm face an additional cost relative to internal shipments. At the same time, they assume internal shipments save on contract costs but impose additional firm governance or management costs. In such a setup, when combined with heterogeneity in overall cost structures, the relationship between productivity and the decision to trade internally or at arms length depends on the trade-off between these various costs. With an appropriate range of parameters, firms with low overall productivity serve only the local market, firms with more intermediate costs serve foreign markets through arm's-length or unaffiliated trade, while the most efficient firms serve distant markets through intrafirm exports.

While the recent body of theory on firms and trade focuses on goods producing firms, the same basic theoretical framework also promises valuable insights for service firms, once we reinterpret physical transport costs as distance costs following from the proximity burden. The first insight relates to "natural" elements of firm costs (those outside policy). Where the most efficient firms engage in internal trade and FDI, since in heterogeneous firm models market share primarily goes to the more efficient firms, we should see most cross-border services trade taking place within MNEs rather than through unaffiliated sales. Going further, establishment sales should be more important than unaffiliated sales for the same reasons. Another insight relates to the impact of policy. In the theoretical literature, internalization hinges on a mix of costs affecting internal and armslength delivery, as well as multiplant versus single plant costs and distance costs. If we map these to the different modes of supply, concessions made in trade agreements or unilateral changes in national policies that affect these different costs should affect the choice of modes, the importance of establishment sales, and the importance of armslength versus internal cross-border sales, in predictable ways. This suggests potentially fruitful application of the recent theory on goods-producing MNEs and internalization of transactions to formulate questions that map nicely to patterns in the services trade and policy data.

3. Market Structure, Tasks, and Fragmentation

Scale economies, imperfect competition, and product differentiation all carry implications for growth and the gains from trade. Markusen (1989) has emphasized the role of increased specialization in producer services as a source of gains from trade in services. This implies gains from increased varieties of services and expanded markets. It has been an important mechanism for estimated gains from trade in the empirical literature reviewed in the next section. Even lacking externalities in the service sector, trade may still support productivity growth in manufacturing. For example, Oulton (2001) has shown that this may increase overall growth, because greater outsourcing of services by (productive) firms in nonstagnant sectors entails a reallocation of factors that increase overall output and aggregate productivity. Along similar lines, Fixler and Siegel (1999) argue that outsourcing of services by manufacturing firms may show up in the short term divergences in measured productivity growth of services versus manufacturing sectors.

The literature also highlights productivity linkages between the organization of production (tasks) within firms and the role of services in making possible the process of offshoring (Peter Debaere, HolgerGorg, and Horst Raff 2009). Francois (1987, 1990a) offers a formal model of nested tasks based on the Brian K. Edwards and Ross M. Starr (1987) characterization of division of labor in production. Services serve a coordination role and make possible a further subdivision of tasks and wholesale reorganization of production, leading to economies of scale. Jones and Kierzkowski (1990) offer a less formal analysis of the same issue. Given the emphasis of this literature on the role of producer services in the organization of production, the support of division of labor in manufacturing provides an additional vector for growth effects. Other papers along these lines include Paolo Guerrieri et al. (2005) with a theoretical analysis that includes the role of greater competition in producer services as a driver of economic growth, Robin Burgess and Anthony J. Venables (2004) who identify the importance of a variety of services "inputs" that support specialization, creation and diffusion of knowledge, and exchange; and Robert-Nicoud (2008), who develops a model in which declining communications costs attenuate agglomeration externalities and allow specialization in production and export of "routine" services tasks in low income countries.

Historically, many service industries have been characterized by a mix of network externalities (telecommunications, finance, transportation), heavy regulation (communications, insurance, professional services), and both natural and policy barriers to entry. This is also true, of course, in many goods sectors. However, in the case of services, the sectors involved are often "margin sectors," meaning they facilitate transactions between agents though transport, communications, trade, and intermediation activities (Deardorff 2001). This implies potential market power both downstream through oligopoly or monopoly pricing, and upstream through oligopsony or monopsony pricing. Market power then drives a pricing wedge between goods producing firms and their customers, between savers and investors, and between economic agents relying on communications and transport linkages. For these reasons, the theoretical literature on trade and FDI in services have also emphasized the importance of regulation and competition.

One theme highlighted in contributions to this literature is market power in trade and distribution sectors. This is closely related to the recent macroeconomic literature on price pass-through, which also highlights the structure of retail sectors in determining transmission of border prices to consumers and downstream industry. Raff and Nicolas Schmitt (2009) examine the potential for trade liberalization in goods to lead to increased concentration in the retail sectors, while Francois and Ian Wooton (2010) focus on the impact of combined oligopsony/oligopoly pricing in retail and wholesale trade on the gains from trade liberalization. Francois and Wooton (2001a) focus on a related issue, developing a theoretical structure where trade requires transport costs supplied by a shipping sector operating as an oligopoly. In general, the message from this literature is that with intermediate service firms exercising market power on two margins (including retail, wholesale, and transport/logistic firms), the gains from trade in goods hinges on the degree of competition in service sectors, and trade and FDI policy in services may therefore impact directly and substantively on trade in goods.

In addition to cross-sector adjustment issues, the theoretical literature also demonstrates that sequencing of policy reforms may be important because of interactions between market structure and alternative modes of supply within sectors. Francois and Wooton (2001b) introduce this point, examining the interaction between different modes of market access liberalization in services. Their results illustrate one of the ways in which there are interdependencies across modes of supply and the policies affecting the feasibility (cost) of using alternative modes. As the cost of disembodied crossborder trade (mode 1) falls (from negotiated concessions, for example), the incentive for domestic oligopolistic sectors to accommodate foreign competitors through welfarereducing establishment (mode 3) rises. A policy implication is that active domestic competition law enforcement may be beneficial in such instances.

4. Regulation

Regulation in services is pervasive and is driven by both efficiency and equity concerns. The characteristics of many services give rise to market failures. For example, the existence of natural monopoly or oligopoly is a feature of "infrastructure services" that require specialized distribution networks: roads and railways, airports, or cables and satellites for telecommunications. Entry into such activities will often be restricted because of geography and policy. Regulation of the owners/operators of the networks can then enhance efficiency by seeking to preclude prohibitive charges for access or interconnection to their established networks. Problems of imperfect and asymmetric information are frequent in the services context. Buyers (consumers) confront serious hurdles in assessing the quality of service providers—e.g., the competence of professionals such as doctors and lawyers, the safety of transport services, or the soundness of banks and insurance companies. When such information is costly to obtain and disseminate and consumers have similar preferences about the relevant attributes of the service supplier, the regulation of entry and operations in a sector can increase welfare. In addition to efficiency justifications for regulation, governments may regulate to achieve equity objectives—e.g., ensuring access to services for disadvantaged regions, communities or households. Instruments to pursue equity objectives may rely on command and control—e.g., requiring a minimum number of poor households to be served, establishment of a certain number of facilities in specific locations—or on the price mechanism. Examples of the latter are universal access funds that are competitively allocated to providers and used to cover the additional costs of service delivery. The design of efficient regulation is not something on which trade economists have much to say. However, the existence of regulation, and the fact that regulation of the same service differs across countries, can have important implications for the feasibility of trade, the welfare impacts of trade liberalization, and empirical assessments of the size of such impacts.

Part 4 Reading Comprehension 阅读理解

Passage 1 The Factor Proportions Theory 要素禀赋论

The factor proportions theory was originally developed by two Swedish economists, Eli Heckscher and his student Bertil Ohlin in the 1920s. So it is also called the "Heck/cher-Ohlin (H-O) Theory".

The H-O model assumes that the only difference between countries is those differences in the relative endowments of factors of production. It is ultimately shown that trade will occur, trade will be nationally advantageous, and trade will have important effects upon prices, when the nations differ in their relative factor endowments and when different industries use factors in different proportions. In other words, difference in factor endowments between countries is one reason for international trade.

The H-O Theory predicts the pattern of trade between countries based on the characteristics of the countries. The H-O theorem says that a capital-abundant country will export the capital-intensive good while the labor-abundant country will export the labor-intensive good.

Unit 1
International Trade Theories and Policies 国际贸易理论与政策

A capital-abundant country is one that is well-endowed with capital relative to the other country. This gives the country a propensity for producing the good which uses relatively more capital in the production process, i.e. the capital-intensive good. As a result, if these two countries were not trading initially, i.e. they were in autarky, the price of the capital-intensive good in the capital-abundant country would be bid down (due to its extra supply) relative to the price of the good in the other country. Similarly, in the labor-abundant country the price of the labor-intensive good would be bid down relative to the price of that good in the capital-abundant country.

Once trade is allowed, profit-seeking firms will move their products to the markets that temporarily have the higher price. Thus the capital-abundant country will export the capital-intensive good since the price will be temporarily higher in the other country. Likewise the labor-abundant country will export the labor-intensive good. Trades flows will ride until the price of both goods are equalized in the two markets.

It is worth emphasizing here a fundamental distinction between the H-O model and the Ricardian model. Whereas the Ricardian model assumes that production technologies differ between countries, the H-O model assumes that production technologies are the same. The reason for the identical technology assumption in the H-O model, is perhaps not so much because it is believed that technologies are really the same. However, the assumption is very useful because it enables us to see precisely how differences in resource endowments is sufficient to cause trade and it shows what impacts will arise entirely due to these difference.

Questions and Discussion

1. Tell the main point of the factor proportions theory.
2. Discuss the applying of the theory of the factor proportions in the present world.

Passage 2 Intra-industry Trade 产业内贸易理论

Intra-industry trade refers to the exchange of products belonging to the same industry. The term is usually applied to international trade, where the same kinds of products and services are both imported and exported in a particular country.

Examples of this kind of trade include cars, foodstuffs and beverages, computers and minerals. Europe exported 2.6 million motor vehicles in 2002, and imported 2.2 million of them. Japan exported 4.7 million motor vehicles in 2002 (1 million of which went to Europe, and 2million to North America), and imported 0.3 million.

Why do countries at the same time import and export the products of the same industry, or import and export the same kinds of goods? Besides those academic explanations by those economists, Intra-industry trade may occur due to the following simple reasons.

1. Seasonality

For example, in agricultural products, such as English apples, which may be exported all around the world during a particularly good apple growing season, but imported during a poor one.

2. Transport Costs

Firms in two adjoining countries with a long border may find it more cost effective to trade with neighboring country goods which it already produces domestically. For example, in country A, firm A1 can trade with firm A2, however, firm B1 (although it is located in another country B) is closer. Transport costs for goods between the two firms of A1 and B1 are therefore less, and Intra-industry trade may occur.

3. Economies of Scale

Internal economies of scale may lead to a firm to specialize in a narrow product line (to produce the large volume necessary for economies of scale benefits); other firms in other countries may focus on producing products that are similarly narrow, yet extremely similar. This is product differentiation. If consumers in either country want to buy both products, they will be importing and exporting. For example, both U.S. and Japan produce cars. The U.S. cars are often luxury and running fast while Japanese cars are often economical and gasoline-saving. There are some customers like Japanese cars in U.S. and some customers like U.S. cars in Japan. So U.S. and Japan trade cars with each other.

External economies of scale could also be used to explain some phenomena in international trade. A country may dominate world market in a particular product, not because it has one or two massive firms producing enormous quantities, but rather because it has many small firms that interact to create a large, competitive industry (for example, five medium-sized crystal glassware manufacturers in eastern Germany).

However, Intra-industry trade is difficult to measure statistically because regarding products or industries as the "same" is partly a matter of definition and classification. For a very simple example, it could be argued that although a BMW and a Ford are both motor cars, and although a Budweiser and a Heineken are both beers, they are really all different products.

Questions and Discussion

1. Tell the main point of the intra-industry trade theory.
2. Discuss the applying of the intra-industry trade theory in the present world.

Unit 1 International Trade Theories and Policies 国际贸易理论与政策

Part 5 课文注释

1. It did not take long, however, for him to realize that there were some things he was more capable of doing than others and that it would benefit him to concentrate his efforts on the production of those goods in which he was particularly proficient and leave others to produce the goods that called for skills which he did not possess. This was the beginning of specialization.

翻译：不久人们就意识到，有些事情他能比别人做得更好，而且，假如他集中精力生产那些他擅长生产的商品，而让别人去生产那些需要他们所不具备的技能的商品，这样他们就有利可图了。这就是分工的开始。

2. Nations will usually produce and export those goods in which they have the greatest comparative advantage, and import those items in which they have the least comparative advantage.

翻译：各国通常生产并出口他们具有比较优势的产品，而进口那些他们不具比较优势的产品。

3. Product life-cycle theory suggests that long-term patterns of international trade are influenced by product innovation and subsequent diffusion.

翻译：产品生命周期理论认为，长期来看，产品创新及其扩散会影响国际贸易格局。

Part 6 词汇及扩展

absolute advantage 绝对优势
comparative advantage 比较优势
the Factor-endowment Theory 要素禀赋论
factor of production 生产要素
labor/capital intensive 劳动/资本密集型的
technology intensive 技术密集型的
the Product Life-cycle Theory 产品生命周期理论
internal/external economies of scale 内部/外部规模经济
intra-industry trade 产业内贸易
product differentiation 产品差异化
Manchesterism 保护贸易主义
Trade Policy Review Body 贸易政策审议机制

Dispute Settlement Body 贸易争端解决机制
Most favored Nation treatment 最惠国待遇
National treatment 国民待遇
specific tariff 从量税
ad valorem tariff 从价税
alternative tariff 选择税
compound tariff 混合税
preferential tariff 特惠税
quota 配额
countertrade 对销贸易
barter 易货贸易
Clearing Agreement 清偿协议
export/import pre-shipment inspection 出港/进港检查
Consular Invoice 领事发票
Currency Deposit in Importations 存款保证金
Government Procurement Policy 政府采购政策
countervailing tariff 反补贴税
anti-dumping tariff 反倾销税
absolute quota 绝对配额
tariff quota 关税配额
country quota 国别配额
global quota 全球配额
voluntary export restriction 自动出口限制
foreign exchange control 外汇管制
persistent dumping 持续性倾销
sporadic dumping 偶然性倾销
predatory dumping 掠夺性倾销

Part 7 网络学习资源

1. 世界贸易组织的网站提供了许多关于李嘉图的简要传记、作品和资料，以及最近世界贸易研究的信息，可以登录 http://www.wto.org。

International Trade Theories and Policies 国际贸易理论与政策

2. 到联合国主页上查找一些贸易相关的数据，登录 www.un.org/depts/unsd/mbsreg.htm。

3. 美国商业部国际贸易管理署的主页按世界、地区和国家提供了各国的各种贸易统计数据，可以登录 www.ita.doc.gov/td/industry/otea/。

4. 美国劳动统计局的国外劳动力统计社对美国和其他国家个人的劳动报酬进行统计和比较，网址为 www.bls.gov/flsdata.htm。

5. 要获得欧盟一些国家的贸易壁垒数据，可以登录 http://mkaccdb.eu.int。

6. 想了解一个国家的国际贸易和关税前景，可以登录 www.mft.govt.nz/for.html。

Unit 2   International Trade Practices
国际贸易实务

Part 1   Intensive Reading   精读

Passage 1   The Export Sales Contract 出口销售合同

The formulation of the export sales contract represents the conclusion of some possibly difficult negotiations and accordingly, particular care should be taken regarding the preparation of its terms. It must be borne in mind that an exporter's primary task is to sell his products at a profit and, therefore, the contract should fulfill this objective insofar as his obligations are concerned. *Above all, they should be capable of being executed under reasonable circumstances and ultimately produce a modest profit. It is, of course, realized that, in the initial stages of developing a new market overseas, a loss may be incurred, but with the long-term marketing plan objective to increase the market share it should ultimately gain a favorable profit level.* A further point to bear in mind is that the export sales contract also embraces a further contract as found in the delivery terms which may be CIF, EX-Works, FOB, etc.

Details of a typical UK export contract are given below, but it must be stressed that they differ by individual country.

(1) The exporter's /seller's registered name and address.

(2) The importer's /buyer's registered name and address.

(3) A short title of each party quoted in items (1) and (2).

(4) Purpose of the contract. For example, it should confirm the specified merchandise is sold by the party detailed in item (1) to the addressee quoted in item (2), and that the latter has bought according to the terms and conditions laid down in the contract.

(5) The quality and quantity of goods precisely and fully described to avoid any later misunderstanding or dispute. In particular, one must mention details of any batches and reconcile goods description with customs tariff specification.

(6) Price. This may be quoted in sterling depending on its stability or some other currency which is not likely to vary in value significantly throughout the contract duration such as American dollars or euros. *To counter inflation, particularly in a long-term contract, it is usual to incorporate*

an escalation clause therein, and to reduce the risk of sterling fluctuations implications, the tendency is to invoice in foreign currencies.

(7) Terms of delivery, for example, CIF Lagos, FOB London, EX-Works Luton. There is an increasing tendency for many importers, particularly those situated in Third World countries to insist on the goods being conveyed by their own national airline or shipping company. It is important both parties to the contract fully understand their obligations as the interpretation of the terms of delivery can sometimes vary by individual country. The ideal solution is to quote Incoterms which are generally recognized worldwide.

(8) Terms of payment, for example, open account, cash with order, sight bills or term bills. Again, this requires careful consideration. Many importers today require extended credit and the exporter's local bank manager should be able to give the requisite guidance on this matter.

(9) Delivery date/shipment date or period. The exporter should check with his production department the delivery date quoted is realistic and the shipping or air freight space will be available on the date or period specified. The exporter's obligations regarding the latter will depend on the terms of delivery.

(10) Methods of shipment, for example, container, train, ferry, Ro/Ro and air freight.

(11) Method of packing. It is desirable both parties are fully aware and agree of the packing specification to ensure no dispute later arises regarding packing or any variation to it.

(12) Insurance-policy or cover note terms.

(13) Import or export license details or other instructions. The period of their validity must be reconciled with the terms of payment and delivery date/shipment date.

(14) Shipping/freight/documentary requirements and/or instructions. This includes marking of cargo.

(15) Contract condition, for example, sale, delivery, quality of goods, arbitration, etc. With regard to arbitration, it is preferable to speed settlement of any disputes without costly litigation.

(16) Signature. Both parties are to sign the contract each by a responsible person who may be at directorial or managerial level, and the date recorded.

A copy of the contract should be retained by each party.

Passage 2 Shipping, Insurance and Customs 海运保险和海关

1. Shipping

The most important shipping document is the bill of lading. It is : firstly, a contract between the shipper and the shipping company ; secondly, a receipt for the consignment; and thirdly, a document of title. A bill of lading doesn't only contain a full description of the consignment—numbers and weights and marks of packages—but a lot of other information as well. It quotes the name of the shipper and the carrying vessel, the ports of shipment and destination, the freight rate, the name of the consignee (unless the B/L is "to order", like a cheque), and the date of shipment, which is very important from a contractual point of view.

It may also contain a number of other clauses. Some bill of lading are marked "freight paid", when a shipper is selling C.I.F or C.&F., others may allow transshipment, which means that the cargo may be transferred from one ship to another at some intermediate port. It is often important to a shipper that his bill of lading should be "clean" rather than "dirty": that is, that the shipping company should not have made any qualifications about the quantity or condition of the cargo actually shipped. *This is because the shipper's letter of credit may insist on clean bills, just as it may insist on "on-board" as opposed to "alongside" bladings. Sometimes a mate's receipt is given to the shipper in advance of the B/L, which takes time to issue.*

Normally four copies of a bill of lading are issued. Two copies will be signed by the ship's master or his agent, two remaining unsigned. The shipper then sends one signed and one unsigned copy to his consignee by airmail, and other pair, by seamail. He can also ask for extra copies for his files. If you ship in a container—one of those standard, giant package loaded on special container vessels—there are a few differences in the way consignments are documented.

2. Insurance

The export trade is subject to many risks. Ships may sink or consignments be damaged in transit, exchange rates may alter, buyers default or governments suddenly impose an embargo.

Exporters can insure themselves against many of these risks. The cover paid for will vary according to the type of goods and the circumstances; delicate goods, such as breakable crockery, cotton piece goods or perishable foodstuffs, obviously have to be covered against more risks than sturdy articles like steel girders.

Insurance brokers will quote rates for all types of cargo and risks. In London they may place their business though Lloyd's, the centre of marine insurance which started in a seventeenth-century coffee house. Regular shippers may take out a floating policy which gives automatic cover for a fixed maximum value of shipments, based on the previous year's trade, provided each shipments is declared when made. *Open cover is an even more flexible type of insurance, limited to twelve months, at agreed terms and rates. In both these case a certificate of insurance is issued instead of a policy. Aviation insurance follows marine insurance very closely, but on the whole is much cheaper.*

3. Customs

Customs authorities work closely with the central bank to ensure that goods are only imported or exported in accordance with current regulations. They have to levy duty, where applicable, on a weight or quantity basis, or ad valorem; and they must verify, to prevent dumping and the illegal transfer of funds outside the country, that the goods are being sold at the current market rate ruling in the country of origin.

Customs entries are required for both imports and exports. Some articles or commodities may be actually shipped before an entry is submitted; in this case the shipping note sent to the wharfinger will be marked "pre-entry not required".

Consular invoices are declaration made at the consular of the importing country. They confirm the ex works cost of a consignment. One copy is sent to the importing customs, another accompanies documents presented through a bank. Sometimes, however, all that needed is a certificate of value endorsed by a chamber of commerce, and combined with enable the importing customs to assess consignments at the correct rate of duty.

Passage 3 Settling of Trade Disputes 国际贸易争端的解决

Disputes in international trade refer to a case in which one party of a business transaction accuses the other of nor having fulfilled its obligation in accordance with the provisions of the contract. There are several ways of settling an international trade dispute. In general, the two parties may either conduct direct consultation to sole the dispute (amicable settlement), or settle the dispute by means of conciliation, arbitration, and litigation.

Amicable settlement. Amicable settlement, i.e. negotiating a solution between the two parties, without outside intervention, is a faster and less expensive method to settle a trade dispute. An overwhelming majority of the disputes has been solved through amicable negotiations and friendly business relations maintained between the buyer and the seller.

Arbitration. Arbitration is a means of settling disputes between the two parties, upon mutual agreement, by the impartial decision of a third party. The decision on the dispute is final and compulsory.

Conciliation. Upon agreement between the parties involved in a dispute, a third party may be invited to interfere. *The difference between conciliation and arbitration is that the award of arbitration is final and compulsory whereas opinions of the conciliator are only for the reference of the two sides, and not compulsory.*

Litigation. One of the parties concerned may refer a dispute to the court which will make a judgment according the law. This is what people call "going through the court". The difference between litigation and arbitration is that the plain-till may take unilateral action without agreement between the two parties in advance. According to usual practice, the court, except under particular circumstances, will generally not accept a case if the two sides have an arbitration agreement.

Part 2 Extensive Reading 泛读

Passage 1 A Sample of Sales Contract 出口合同样本

No:

Date:

For Account of:

Indent No:

This contract is made by and between the Sellers and the Buyers; Whereby the Sellers agree to sell and the Buyers agree to buy the under mentioned goods according to the terms and conditions stipulated below and overleaf:

(1) Names of commodity (ies) and specification(s)

(2) Quantity

(3) Unit price

(4) Amount

TOTAL:

_____% more or less allowed.

(5) Packing:

(6) Port of Loading:

(7) Port of Destination:

(8) Shipping Marks:

(9) Time of Shipment: Within _____ days after receipt of L/C, allowing transshipment and partial shipment.

(10) Terms of Payment:

By 100% Confirmed, Irrevocable and Sight Letter of Credit to remain valid for negotiation in China until the 15th day after shipment.

(11) Insurance:

Covers all risks and war risks only as per the Clauses of the People's Insurance Company of China for 110% of the invoice value. To be effected by the Buyer.

(12) The Buyer shall establish the covering Letter of Credit before _____; failing which,

the Seller reserves the right to rescind this Sales Contract without further notice, or to accept whole or any part of this Sales Contract, non-fulfilled by the Buyer, of to lodge claim for direct losses sustained, if any.

(13) Documents: The Sellers shall present to the negotiating bank, Clean On Board Bill of Lading, Invoice, Quality Certificate issued by the China Commodity Inspection Bureau or the Manufacturers, Survey Report on Quantity/Weight issued by the China Commodity Inspection Bureau, and Transferable Insurance policy or Insurance Certificate when this contract is made on CIF basis.

(14) For this contract signed on CIF basis, the premium should be 110% of invoice value. All risks insured should be included within this contract. If the Buyer asks to increase the insurance premium or scope of risks, he should get the permission of the Seller before time of loading, and all the charges thus incurred should be borne by the Buyer.

(15) Quality/Quantity Discrepancy; In case of quality discrepancy, claim should be filed by the Buyer within 30 days after the arrival of the goods at port of destination; while for quantity discrepancy, claim should be filed by the Buyer within 15 days after the arrival of the goods at port of destination. It is understood that the Seller shall not be liable for any discrepancy of the goods shipped due to causes for which the Insurance Company, Shipping Company, other transportation organizations and/or Post Office are liable.

(16) The Seller shall not be held liable for failure or delay in delivery of the entire lot or a portion of the goods under this Sales Contract in consequence of any Force Majeure incidents.

(17) Arbitration:

All disputes in connection with this contract or the execution thereof shall be settled friendly through negotiations. In case no settlement can be reached, the case may then be submitted for arbitration to China International Economic and Trade Arbitration Commission in accordance with the provisional Rules of Procedures promulgated by the said Arbitration Commission. The arbitration shall take place in Beijing and the decision of the Arbitration Commission shall be final and binding upon both parties; neither party shall seek recourse to a law court nor other authorities to appeal for revision of the decision. Arbitration fee shall be borne by the losing party. Or arbitration may be settled in the third country mutually agreed upon by both parties.

(18) The Buyer is requested always to quote THE NUMBER OF THE SALES CONTRACT in the Letter of Credit to be opened in favor of the Seller.

(19) Other Conditions:

Seller: Buyer:

Passage 2 Issues Affecting International Contracts 影响国际商务合同的种种问题

Success in foreign trade depends on how flexible you are in recognizing and respecting the culture of other people. In a business context, culture is a set of rules that govern the way in which commercial transactions are conducted between people from different countries. These rules dictate etiquette, traditions, values, communication, and negotiating styles and so you have to be sensitive to other cultures and adapt. Culture applies to people and not necessarily countries and so it is important not to rely on preconceived notions you have about a country. Cultural awareness is most important in the initial contact and negotiation because after that you may figure out the rules. At first you have to understand whether or not the general protocol in the country is rigidly applied. Then you have to determine what the protocol is for the counter negotiations. It is important to ensure that you are approaching cultural issues with the proper attitude. Cultural missteps are inevitable and you must be able to laugh at yourself and bring humor into the situation as this will ease tension.

Very many trade agreements have come about in the last decade, such as the General Agreement on Trade and Tariffs (GATT) and the North American Free Trade Agreement (NAFTA). Many countries have come to realize that development and refinement of a global economic strategy is important to the growth and maintenance of a strong economy. Much of the pressure for this has come from the private business sector. This encourages the trend toward a uniform international law of commerce in recognition of the difficulties of applying national laws across country borders.

United Nation has made Convention on Contracts for the International Sale of Goods (CIGS). The CIGS was finalized at the UN convention in 1980 but went into effect in the member countries at different times. Member countries are entitled to accede to the CIGS with reservations and many of them have chosen to exclude the application of certain provisions. The main objectives of CIGS was: to adopt rules governing international contracts, to set uniform rules accounting foe different social, economic, and legal systems, to help remove legal barriers in international trade, and to promote international trade.

Political events have a major impact on economics. Instability can be devastating while stability in government can be a great asset. A strong economy can then have a claiming effect on political turmoil. In the past, governments have used trade barriers to force change in the governments and policies of other countries. These include boycotts, quotas, tariffs, prohibitions, licenses, requirements and regulations. Favorable trade preferences have been granted to countries that implement changes thought to be desirable. As an international trader you must stay in touch with political trends. The stability of a region will indicate whether you will succeed long term there.

It is your responsibility to know the legal implications and boundaries of trading in your country and abroad. An attorney with international experience can give you some advice.

Passage 3 Trade Facilitation and Promotion 贸易便捷化与贸易促进

1. Trade Facilitation and Documentation

Trade facilitation is an important export support service that could be provided by the TPO. Trade facilitation is defined as the simplification and harmonization of international trade procedures, with trade procedures being the activities, practices and formalities involved in collecting, presenting, communicating and processing data required for the movement of goods in international trade. This definition relates to a wide range of activities, such as import and export procedures (customs or licensing procedures); transport formalities; and payments, insurance and other financial requirements. In general, the focus should be on the smooth and rapid movement of a country's products to the outside world and the smooth and rapid movement of important inputs reaching important sectors of the domestic market. The lack of an efficient trade facilitation mechanism will impede both imports and exports. The basis of any trade facilitation is a transparent and strong legal framework. Clear regulations on the process and application procedures for imports and exports should be defined and closely follow international practices. The legal framework must establish the regulatory authority or authorities and the scope of their authority.

Trade procedures have to be transparent in order to be effective. This will require efforts by the import/export regulatory body to actively disseminate the regulations to traders and give updates on any regulatory changes. Proper documentation and clear procedures are necessary to facilitate the traffic and transit of products in and out the country.

Procedures must be well documented and widely disseminated. It is common for most government departments and agencies to have their own documentation forms. However, this creates problems for traders who have to visit each authority separately to clarify the information required in the forms. The TPO should ensure that such documentation and procedures are simplified.

2. Export Financing

The promotion of exports requires strong financial support and assistance. The absence of an efficient financial system will be a serious constraint for exporters. In particular, first-time exporters will need facilities like trade financing, export insurance and financial guarantees.

Financing, insurance and guarantees for exports are services covered by almost all TPOs in developed countries and by about 60 per cent of those in developing countries. There is a close relationship between financing and successfully completing an export deal. Many export deals fail due to inadequate funding. In many cases, it is not because of the lack of appropriate funding sources, but from lack of knowledge about funding sources and how exporters can gain access to them. Export credit insurance agencies in the public sector usually cover both commercial and political risk in the broadest sense of the terms. They are willing to insure an exporter against the risk of non-payment on the due date specified in the sales contract, ①in the case of a "supplier credit"; that is, when the exporter gives the importer a period of time to pay for the goods, with or without a credit from the exporter's own bank; or ②when a bank finances the export operation in the case of a "buyer credit", when the exporter's bank provides credit directly to the importer. The risk of non-payment may occur in two cases.

(1) When a private buyer in the importing country is not able to make the required payment (deposit) in the local currency to his central bank (or a commercial bank).

(2) When the buyer in the importing country has deposited the payment in local currency, but his country is not able to convert that amount into hard currency (a political or country risk).

With more people trading across borders, payments systems and cultures, payment for exports is as vital as ever and increasingly complicated. There are four main methods of payment for exports depending on the size and circumstances of a company.

(1) Cash in advance - the ideal.

(2) Open account - if you know your buyer well.

(3) Collect on Delivery - more security where you have yet to establish a relationship.

(4) Letters of credit - security for the buyer and seller.

Guarantees are normally granted by financing institutions to support the productive capabilities of exporters. For example, guarantees can be used to import machinery and equipment. In the case of machine imports, a bank can guarantee the payment for the machinery. Governments can play a proactive role to support trading activities. This is especially for cases with trading partners, whose exporters are not familiar with the region or are concerned about payment. They can through their central banks set up a trade financing scheme where the central banks will guarantee the letter of credits issued by their local banks. This trade-financing scheme is envisaged to be short term mechanism just to initiate trade activities with new trading partners. Once confidence has developed between both sides, the trade-financing scheme can be stopped.

(1) Assistance to Solve Financial Problems

Lack of knowledge about the sources of financing to cover export operations is one of the biggest problems faced by exporters in developing countries. This creates complications and prevents exporters from being more actively involved in the export trade. Therefore, the TPO, together with the government, should consider ways and means to overcome the constraints in export financing. As part of their export support services, TPOs could provide help in solving exporters' financial problems, through proper guidance in the right types of financial assistance and the handling of credit applications. It is necessary to have a specialist to give assistance in solving financial problems. This person must have thorough knowledge of:

① Entities which provide financing for production and export purposes.
② Conditions governing terms, interest rates, guarantees and insurance.
③ The general volume of resources available for credit operations.

The specialist must be able to do the following.

(a) Contact various financial institutions (commercial and development banks) to identify the conditions of their credit operations. This should include identifying the documentation required, the rate of interest charged and the terms for required guarantees of repayment.

(b) Form an export finance "contact group" with the financial institutions so that they become an advisory body to the TPO; develop expertise in completing application forms; and identify possibilities in the country for financing the various stages in the export process, including pre-shipment and post-shipment. The search for information should include the central bank and identify the bank's policies on rediscount facilities.

(c) Prepare information that summarizes and gives details about the existing conditions and sources of financial resources and guarantees for exporters. This information should be gathered in consultation with the financial community/contact group to assure its accuracy. Credit manuals might be a convenient way to disseminate this information to interested parties. The manuals should be in language understandable to the non-professional. When applicable, special privileges granted to exporters as part of available credit operations must be pointed out.

(d) Provide on-the-spot general advice to exporters about possible solutions to their funding needs as well as help on how to complete credit applications. For specific detailed information and advice, the specialist should arrange for the exporter to meet the relevant financial institutions.

(e) Identify specific and general problems related to credit and guarantee regulations that may affect the export sector, make a careful study and then formulate recommendations for solutions. Information on the financial systems of other countries could provide a comparison in order to recommend solutions.

(f) Organize seminars and workshops in order to educate and update exporters on developments in export finance and counter trade.

(g) Guide interested parties to the best sources of technical assistance for doing feasibility studies and other studies, which are required for certain credit arrangements.

(h) Arrange to introduce exporters to the credit and financial institutions relevant to their needs.

(2) Functions of a Financial Specialist

Assistance must be provided in a systematic manner to exporters who are not familiar with existing mechanisms. There is, therefore, a need for a specialist in the TPO who has a thorough understanding of the sources and mechanisms for export financing. Some basic functions of a TPO financial specialist are to:

① Help manufacturers and exporters to obtain adequate credit coverage for their export operations.

② Help exporters to fill out questionnaires and application forms required by credit institutions.

③ Guide interested parties to the best sources of technical assistance for doing feasibility studies and other studies which are required for certain credit arrangements.

④ Identify any critical shortcomings in financial facilities by contacting exporters and other TPO staff.

⑤ Study credit and finance systems in other countries at similar or comparable stages of development and draw on their experience with credit problems in order to recommend improvements that will make local exporters more competitive.

(3) Export Financing Instruments

The following list covers the main types of export financing instruments.

① Countertrade.

There are many forms of countertrade, including:

a. Barter, which is the exchange of goods and services for other goods and services of equivalent value, with no monetary exchange between exporter and importer.

b. Counter purchase is when the exporter undertakes to buy goods from the importer or from a company nominated by the importer or agrees to arrange for the purchase by a third party. The value of the counter purchased goods is an agreed percentage of the prices of the goods originally exported.

c. Buy-back is where the exporter of heavy equipment agrees to buy products manufactured by the importer. Countertrade offers a feasible option for Central Asian economies endowed with rich natural resources like oil and grain. For countries with either surrender requirements on foreign earnings or lack of currency convertibility, countertrade can be the first step towards export expansion.

② Documentary credit.

This is the most common form of the commercial letter of credit. A common problem is that many local banks in developing countries have inadequate capital and therefore do not have the ability to back documentary credits. Exporters may require confirmation by their own local banks as an additional source of security, but this creates additional costs, and the banks may not want to assume the risks.

③ Factoring.

This is the sale of accounts receivable or other assets at a discount on a daily, weekly or monthly basis in exchange for immediate cash. The exporter sells the assets at a discount to a factoring house, which assumes all commercial and political risks.

④ Pre-shipping financing.

This is financing for the period prior to the shipment of goods, to support pre-export wages and overhead costs. It is needed especially when production inputs must be imported. Preshipment financing is important to smaller enterprises, because the international sales cycle is usually longer than domestic sales cycle. Pre-shipment financing can be in the form of short-term loans, overdrafts, and cash credits.

⑤ Post-shipping financing.

This is financing for the period following shipment. The ability to be competitive often depends on the credit terms that the exporter offers to buyers. Post-shipment financing is usually short-term.

⑥ Buyer's credit.

This is a financial arrangement where a lending bank, financial institution, or an export credit agency in the exporting country extends a loan directly to a foreign buyer. The loan may also be indirect through a bank in the buyer's country acting on his behalf to finance the purchase of goods and services from the exporting country. It enables the buyer to make payments due to the supplier under the contract.

⑦ Supplier's credit.

This is a financing arrangement under which an exporter extends credit to the buyer in the importing country to finance the buyer's purchases.

3. Export Credit Insurance

Credit insurance is a specialized form of insurance against non-payment of trade debts, when such non-payment arises from commercial or political risks. Under commercial risk, coverage is provided in the event the buyer becomes insolvent, fails to pay, or refuses to take delivery of goods for no justifiable reason. An exporter, however, also faces risks such as war or political disturbances in the buyer's country, blockage or delay in the transfer of funds and imposition of import restrictions or cancellation of the import license. Export credit insurance involves insuring exporters against such risks. It is commonly used in Europe and is increasingly important in the United States of America as well as in developing markets. With export credit insurance, should any event occur making payment impossible, a claim is payable under the policy. The types of export credit insurance used differ among countries and according to the needs of enterprises. The most commonly used types include:

(1) Short-term export credit insurance covers periods not more than 180 days. Protection covers preshipment and post-shipment risks, the former covering the period between the awarding of contracts until shipment. Protection can also be offered against commercial and political risks.

(2) Medium and long-term export credit insurance issued for credits extending for medium-term periods (up to three years) or longer. Protection is provided for financing exports of capital goods and services.

(3) Investment insurance is offered to exporters investing in foreign countries.

(4) Exchange risk insurance covers losses from fluctuations in exchange rate between exporters' and importers' national currencies over a period of time. The benefits of credit insurance include:

① Exporters ability to offer buyers competitive payment terms.

② Protection against risks and financial costs of nonpayment.

③ Access to working capital.

④ Protection from foreign exchange losses and fluctuations.

⑤ Reduction of the need for tangible security when borrowing from banks.

Export credit insurance lessens the financial impact of risks. There are specialized financial institutions that offer insurance, with premiums depending on the risk of the export markets and export products. Export credit insurance agencies act as a bridge between banks and exporters. Byalleviating the financial impact of risks that exporters face, they make banks more assured of exporters' ability to repay loans. Governments traditionally assume the role of credit insurance agents, because they are considered to be the only institutions in a position to bear political risks. For emerging economies where the financial sector is still developing, the government, or a government agent, has the responsibility to act as the export credit insurance agent.

Part 3 Academic Reading 学术阅读

Passage Measures of Trade Restrictiveness 贸易限制的测量

To show how difficult it is to measure a country's trade restrictiveness, I examine a number of situations that illustrate problems with existing measures and provide the foundation for understanding the advances associated with trade restrictiveness indices.

1. A Very Simple Case

The measurement of trade restrictiveness is straightforward when there is only one imported good and a tariff is applied. Figure 2.1 illustrates this simple case. The import demand for this good is represented by D^M. The price in world markets for this good is P_W, which is the price faced by domestic producers and consumers prior to the imposition of the tariff. Thus, the quantity of imports is M_W.

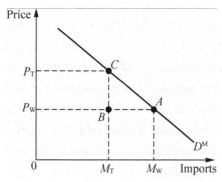

Figure 2.1 One Imported Good Subject to Tariff

Now assume a tariff is imposed that raises the price faced by domestic producers and consumers to P_T. As a result of the higher price, imports would decrease to M_T. The deadweight loss caused by the tariff is represented by the triangle ABC. The restrictiveness of this tariff is simply the height of the tariff, which is the difference between P_T and P_W. Trade restrictiveness increases the difference between the domestic price and the price in world markets. This simplicity vanishes, however, when assessing trade restrictiveness with two or more goods and tariffs.

2. Problems with Existing Measures

Let's begin with a case of two goods that are subjected to different tariffs. One approach could be to construct a measure of trade restrictiveness by computing the simple (i.e., unweighted) average of the two tariff rates. An obvious problem here is that all goods are treated identically. Intuitively, the goods should be weighted in terms of their importance. One common weighting approach is to use actual import volumes as weights. Unfortunately, such an approach is flawed. When a uniform tariff is imposed on all the goods in question, the calculation of an average tariff weighted by import volumes generates a reasonable index: that a higher average tariff accurately indicates a more restrictive policy. However, with a differentiated tariff structure, goods subject to high tariffs will tend to receive lower weight than goods subject to low tariffs. The reason is that the price of a good with a high tariff will tend to rise relative to a good with a low tariff, so consumers will tend to substitute the good with the low tariff for the one with the high tariff. As a result, in the calculation of the import-weighted average tariff, goods with high tariffs will tend to receive less weight than goods with low tariffs. This would tend to reduce the value of the index, which is precisely the opposite of what seems reasonable.

Using Figures 2.2 and 2.3, let's examine more closely the usefulness of an average tariff weighted by import volumes. Identical to the preceding discussion, we use the case of two goods with different tariffs. In Figure 2.2, the left half of the diagram contains information on good M_1 and the right half on good M_2. Similar to Figure 2.1, the demand for M_1 is represented by D^{M1} and the demand for M_2 is represented by D^{M2}. Note that the quantity of M_1 increases with leftward movements along the horizontal axis and that the quantity of M_2 increases with rightward movements along the horizontal axis. To simplify, but without losing any generality, the price in world markets for both goods is assumed to be P_W. Prior to the imposition of a tariff, P_W is the price faced by domestic producers and consumers for both goods. Thus, the quantity of imports of M_1 is $M1_W$ and of M_2 is $M2_W$.

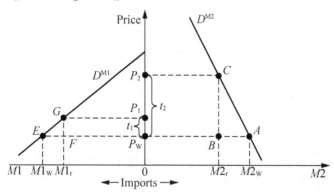

Figure 2.2 Taiff Rates and Import Demand Elasticities: Negative Correlation

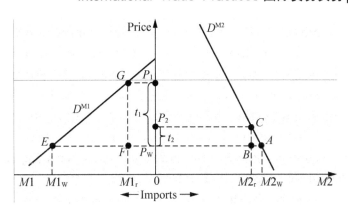

Figure 2.3 Tariff Rates and Import Demand Elasticities: Positive Correlation

Now assume tariffs are imposed such that a lower tariff rate is imposed on the good with the higher price elasticity of import demand (i.e., M_1) than is imposed on the good with the lower price elasticity of import demand (i.e., M_2). In other words, the tariff rate imposed on M_1 is $(P_1 - P_W)/P_W$, while the tariff rate imposed on M_2 is $(P_2 - P_W)/P_W$. Thus, as drawn, there is a negative correlation between the tariff rate and the elasticity. In this case the tariff on M_1 causes the price for domestic consumers and producers to increase to P_1 and the tariff on M_2 causes the price to increase to P_2. As a result, imports would decrease to $M1_T$ and $M2_T$, respectively.

Using Figure 2.2, let t_1 be the specific (i.e., dollar amount) tariff for M_1 and t_2 be the specific tariff for M_2. Then, the trade-weighted average tariff rate, t_w, is: $t_w = (t_1 M1_T + t_2 M2_T)/(P_W M1_T + P_W M2_T)$.

The numerator is the value of tariff revenue, while the denominator is the value of imports using world prices, which were assumed to be identical for the two goods.

Now let's examine Figure 2.3. Once again, the left half contains information on good M_1 and the right half on good M_2, where the demand for M_1 is represented by D^{M1} and the demand for M_2 by D^{M2}. The price in world markets for both goods is assumed to be P_W. Prior to the imposition of a tariff, P_W is the price faced by domestic producers and consumers for both goods. Thus, the quantity of imports of M_1 is $M1_W$ and of M_2 is $M2_W$. Now assume tariffs are imposed such that a higher tariff rate is imposed on the good with the higher price elasticity of import demand (i.e., M_1) than on the good with the lower price elasticity of import demand (i.e., M_2). The tariff rate imposed on M_1 is $(P_1 - P_W)/P_W$, while the tariff rate imposed on M_2 is $(P_2 - P_W)/P_W$. Thus, there is a positive correlation between the tariff rate and the elasticity. In this case, the tariff on M_1 causes the price for domestic consumers and producers to increase to P_1 and the tariff on M_2 causes the price to increase to P_2. As a result, imports would decrease to $M1_T$ and $M2_T$, respectively.

In Figure 2.3, compared with Figure 2.2, imports of M_1 are lower and imports of M_2 are higher. Thus, for the calculation of the trade-weighted average tariff rate, M_1 will receive less weight and M_2 will receive more weight. Moreover, the absolute decrease in the quantity of imports of M_1 exceeds the increase in the quantity of imports of M_2. Recall also that the tariff rate on M_1 (M_2) in Figure 2.3 is the tariff rate on M_2 (M_1) in Figure 2.2. Thus, M_1 (M_2) is subject to a higher (lower) tariff rate in Figure 2.3 than in Figure 2.2. Consequently, the trade-weighted average tariff rate in Figure 2.3 must be less than in Figure 2.2. That trade is more restricted in Figure 2.3 than in Figure 2.2 suggests that the trade-weighted average tariff rate is a flawed measure.

Another way to show that the tariffs in Figure 2.3 are more restrictive than those in Figure 2.2 is to examine the deadweight losses. The deadweight losses in Figure 2.3 exceed those in Figure 2.2. These losses are determined by the sizes of the triangles formed by EFG for good M_1 and by ABC for good M_2. By visual inspection and by mathematics as well, the sum of the areas of EFG and ABC is larger in Figure 2.3 than in Figure 2.2. The economic reason for this result hinges on the correlation between tariff rates and import demand elasticities. For a specific good, the higher (lower) the tariff, the larger (smaller) the deadweight loss. In comparing Figure 2.2 with Figure 2.3, when the higher tariff is switched to the good that is relatively elastic and the lower tariff is switched to the good that is relatively inelastic, then the increase in the deadweight loss associated with M_1 exceeds the decrease in the deadweight loss for M_2. Thus, from the perspective of national well-being, trade restrictiveness is more pronounced for the situation in Figure 2.3 than in Figure 2.2.

3. A Better Way

One suggestion for improving the calculation of the import-weighted average tariff rate is to use the import volumes that would result under free trade to weight tariff rates rather than using the actual imports that result under current trade policy. One attractive feature of such an index is that it necessarily increases when any specific tariff rate is increased. However, because the actual trade flows under free trade are not directly observable, the trade flows and the resulting trade weights must be estimated. It turns out that the information required to estimate free-trade flows is the same as that necessary to estimate "true" indices, which are superior. We now illustrate how to construct an index that is connected to a true index, one based on the welfare or utility impacts of trade policy.

Figure 2.4 uses the same demand curves, prices, and tariff rates as in Figure 2.2. Recall that the tariff rates and the import demand elasticities are selected to be negatively correlated. The specific tariff on good M_1 is $(P_1 - P_W)$ and on good M_2 is $(P_2 - P_W)$. To find the uniform tariff, one must, without changing national well-being, increase the tariff on the good with the lower tariff and decrease the tariff on the good with the higher tariff until the two tariffs are equal. In the present case, the tariff associated with U_1 meets this requirement. When the specific tariff on M1 increases from $(P_1 - P_W)$ to $(U_1 - P_W)$, the decline in welfare (due to the higher price and reduced imports) is represented by the area FGHI. At the same time, when the specific tariff on M_2 decreases from $(P_2 - P_W)$ to $(U_1 - P_W)$, the increase in welfare (due to the lower price and increased imports) is represented by the area BCJK. Thus, the specific tariff, $U_1 - P_W$, is chosen so that the area FGHI equals the area BCJK. The trade restrictiveness index is simply $(U_1 - P_W)/P_W$.

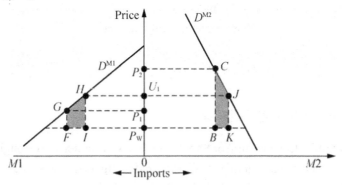

Figure 2.4 Trade restrictiveness indices: Tariff Rates and Import Demand Elasticities Negatively Correlated

Next, Figure 2.5 uses the same demand curves, prices, and tariff rates as in Figure 2.3. Recall that the tariff rates and the import demand elasticities are selected to be positively correlated. The specific tariff on good M_1 is $(P_1 - P_W)$ and on good M_2 is $(P_2 - P_W)$. As noted above, to find the uniform tariff, without changing national well-being, one must increase the tariff on the good with the lower tariff and decrease the tariff on the good with the higher tariff until the two tariffs are equal. In the present case, the tariff associated with U_2 meets this requirement. When the specific tariff on M_1 decreases from $(P_1 - P_W)$ to $(U_2 - P_W)$, the increase in welfare (due to the lower price and increased imports) is represented by the area FGHI. At the same time, when the specific tariff on M_2 increases from $(P_2 - P_W)$ to $(U_2 - P_W)$, the decrease in welfare (due to the higher price and reduced imports) is represented by the area BCJK. Thus, the specific tariff, $(U_2 - P_W)$, is chosen so that the area FGHI equals the area BCJK. The trade restrictiveness index is simply $(U_2 - P_W)/P_W$. Note that, consistent with our previous discussion, the trade restrictiveness index is larger in Figure 2.5 than in Figure 2.4.

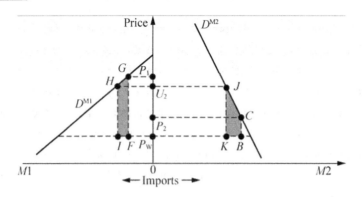

Figure 2.5 Trade restrictiveness indices: Tariff Rates and Import Demand Elasticities Positively Correlated

Part 4 Reading Comprehension 阅读理解

Passage 1 Clinton Is Right 克林顿没错

President Clinton's decision on Apr.8 to send Chinese Premier Zhu Rongji packing without an agreement on China's entry into the World Trade Organization seemed to be a massive miscalculation. The President took a drubbing from much of the press, which had breathlessly reported that a deal was in the bag. The Cabinet and Whit House still appeared divided, and business leaders were characterized as furious over the lost opportunity. Zhu charged that Clinton lacked "the courage" to reach an accord. And when Clinton later telephoned the angry Zhu to pledge a renewed effort at negotiations, the gesture was widely portrayed as a flip-flop.

In fact, Clinton made the right decision in holding out for a better WTO deal. A lot more horse trading is needed before a final agreement can be reached. And without the Administration's goal of a "bullet-proof agreement" that business lobbyists can enthusiastically sell to a Republican Congress, the whole process will end up in partisan acrimony that could harm relations with China for years.

THE HARD PART. Many business lobbyists, while disappointed that the deal was not closed, agree that better terms can still be had. And Treasury Secretary Robert E. Rubin, National Economic Council Director Gene B. Sperling, Commerce Secretary William M. Daley, and top trade negotiator Charlene Barshefsky all advised Clinton that while the Chinese had made a remarkable number of concessions, "we're not there yet," according to senior officials.

Negotiating with Zhu over the remaining issues may be the easy part. Although Clinton can signal U.S. approval for China's entry into the WTO himself, he needs Congress to grant Beijing permanent most-favored-nation status as part of a broad trade accord. And the temptation for meddling on Capital Hill may prove over-whelming. Zhu had barely landed before Senate Majority Leader Trent Lott (R-Miss) declared himself skeptical that China deserved entry into the WTO. And Senators Jesse A. Helms (R-N.C.) and Emest F. Hollings (D-S.C.) promised to introduce a bill requiring congressional approval of any deal.

The hidden message from these three textile-state Southerners: Get more protection for the U.S. clothing industry. Hoping to smooth the way, the Administration tried, but failed, to budge Zhu on textiles. Also left in the lurch: Wall Street, Hollywood, and Detroit. Zhu refused to open up much of the lucrative Chinese securities market and insisted on "cultural" restrictions on American movies and music. He also blocked efforts to allow U.S. auto makers to provide fleet financing.

BIG JOB. Already, business lobbyists are blanketing Capital Hill to presale any eventual agreement, but what they've heard so far isn't encouraging. Republicans, including Lott, say that "the time just isn't right" for the deal. Translation: We're determined to make it look as if Clinton has capitulated to the Chinese and is ignoring human, religious, and labor rights violations; the theft of nuclear-weapons technology; and the sale of missile parts to America's enemies. Beijing's fierce critics within the Democratic Party, such as Senator Paul D. Wellstone of Minnesota and House Minority leader Richard A. Gephardt of Missouri, won't help, either.

Just how tough the lobbying job on Capital Hill will be become clear on Apr. 20, when Rubin lectured 19 chief executives on the need to discipline their Republican allies. With business and the White House still trading charges over who is responsible for the defeat of fast-track trade negotiating legislation in 1997, working together won't be easy. And Republicans—with a wink—say that they'll eventually embrace China's entry into the WTO as a favor to Corporate America. Though not long before they torture Clinton. But Zhu is out on a limb, and if Congress overdoes the criticism, he may be forced by domestic critics to renege. Business must make this much dear to both its GOP allies and the White House: This historic deal is too important to risk losing to any more partisan squabbling.

Questions:

1. The main idea of this passage is (   ).

   [A] The Contradiction between the Democratic Party and the Republican Party

   [B] On China's entry into WTO

   [C] Clinton was right

   [D] Business Lobbyists Control Capital Hill

2. What does the sentence "Also left in the lurch: Wall Street, Hollywood, Detroit" convey? (   )

   [A] Premier Zhu rejected their requirements

   [B] The three places overdid criticism

   [C] They wanted more protection

   [D] They are in trouble

3. What was the attitude of the Republican Party toward China's entry into the WTO? (   )

   [A] Contradictory   [B] Appreciative

   [C] Disapproving   [D] Detestful

4. Who plays the leading part in the deal in America? (   )

   [A] White House   [B] Republicans

   [C] The Democratic Party   [D] Businessmen

5. It can be inferred from the passage that (   ).

   [A] America will make concessions.

   [B] America will hold out for a better WTO

   [C] Clinton has the right to signal U.S. approval for China's entry.

   [D] Democratic party approve China's entry into the WTO.

Passage 2 International Trade and Economic Development 国际贸易与经济发展

Both theory and empirical analysis have well documented the long-term benefits from improved resource allocation and efficiency that follow from trade reform. And, although causation remains an issue, research has also show strong and consistent correlation between reform and growth.

1. Impact on Labor

A survey has been done concerning 50 studies that address the issue of the adjustment costs of trade liberalization, comparing estimates of adjustment with gains from trade liberalization.

Adjustment costs are defined to encompass a wide variety of potentially disadvantageous short-run outcomes that might result from trade liberalization. These outcomes may include a reduction in employment and output, the loss of industry-specific human capital, and macroeconomic instability resulting from balance of payments difficulties or reductions in government revenue.

In addition, the distinction between social and private costs is also important for, while the social costs of adjustment are relevant for considering the aggregate welfare effects of trade reform, it is the distribution of private costs within society that forms the basis of political opposition to reform.

What does this extensive survey indicate? On the whole, and albeit with some caveats, virtually all the studies find that adjustment costs are very small in relation to the benefits of trade liberalization. This is true both in term of the impact of trade reform on employment and its impact on government revenues and macro stability. And those studies that focused on manufacturing employment in developing countries found that it did not decline one year after the introduction of trade liberalization.

The explanation for the low adjustment costs in relation to the benefits is as follows: ①most importantly, adjustment costs are typically short term and terminate when workers find a job, while the benefits of trade reform can be expected to grow with the economy; ②estimate of the duration of unemployment for most industries are not high, especially where workers were not earning substantial rents in original job; ③it has been observed that a great deal of inter-industry shifts occurred after trade liberalization, which minimized the dislocation of factors of production. In addition, developing countries would be expected to have comparative advantage in labor intensive, so trade liberalization should favor labor. This may explain why manufacturing employment has typically increased after trade liberalization.

2. Impact on Industry

One of the main concerns related to import is that opening up to cheaper imports may lead to "deindustrialization". This fear is not unique to developing countries. In the past two decades advanced economics have witnessed a continuous decline in the share of manufacturing employment for which freer trade has sometimes been blamed.

In the context of developing countries, deindustrialization refers to the fear that an open trade policy may lead to the contraction and eventual disappearance of the few manufacturing industries which had often grown behind protective barriers. Although highly protected, import-substituting sectors or at least some firms within the sector, may indeed be forced to live up to foreign competition or shut down, which is precisely what trade reform is supposed to do, the experience of trade reform as a group does not support such fears. On the contrary, countries that have engaged in reform, reducing the anti-export bias of their trade regimes and that have also provided a business-friendly macro and regulatory environment have seen their industrial sector and exports expand. Several East Asian and Latin American countries and some African economies, foremost among then Mauritius, are good examples of this trend. Trade policy reform influence the manufacturing sector and employment in many ways and its impact on productivity, efficiency, labor turnover and so on.

3. Impact on Poverty

Studies on the direct impact of trade reform on poverty are few. To the extent that trade reform improves efficiency and lead to a higher level of income or growth, it is expected to be beneficial to poverty reduction. Also, to the extent that trade reform (broadly defined) reduces anti-export bias and to the extent that exports are intensive in the use of unskilled or rural labor, trade reform is expected to increase the real wage reducing both poverty and inequality.

Part 5　课文注释

1. Above all, they should be capable of being executed under reasonable circumstances and ultimately produce a modest profit. It is, of course, realized that, in the initial stages of developing a new market overseas, a loss may be incurred, but with the long-term marketing plan objective to increase the marker share it should ultimately gain a favorable profit level.

翻译：首要的是，出口商的责任要在适当的情况下能够予以履行，并最后能产生适度的利润。当然，人们意识到在海外发展新市场的初期，可能会有亏损。但是增加市场份额的长期销售计划目标主要是要随后获得有利的利润水平。

2. To counter inflation, particularly in a long-term contract, it is usual to incorporate an escalation clause therein, and to reduce the risk of sterling fluctuations implications, the tendency is to invoice in foreign currencies.

翻译：为了抵消通货膨胀，特别是在一份长期的合同中，通常在里面加上一条价格自动调整条款，为了减少英镑波动的影响，现在的趋势是在发票中采用外国货币。

3. This is because the shipper's letter of credit may insist on clean bills, just as it may insist on "on-board" as opposed to "alongside" bladings. Sometimes a mate's receipt is given to the shipper in advance of the B/L, which takes time to issue.

翻译：这是因为发货人的信用证可能一定要求清洁提单，正像要求"已装船提单"而不同意"备运提单"一样。有时在签发提单以前，先给发货人一张大副收据，因为签发提单得花费一些时间。

4. The export trade is subject to many risks. Ships may sink or consignments be damaged in transit, exchange rates may alter, buyers default or governments suddenly impose an embargo.

翻译：出口贸易常常遇到一些风险，例如船舶可能沉没，货物可能在运输中受损，外汇兑换率可能有变动，买主可能违约或者政府部门突然宣布禁运。

5. Open cover is an even more flexible type of insurance, limited to twelve months, at agreed terms and rates. In both these case a certificate of insurance is issued instead of a policy. Aviation insurance follows marine insurance very closely, but on the whole is much cheaper.

翻译：预约保险是一种灵活性更大的保险类别，根据商定的条件和费用限于12个月内有效。在上述两种情况下，发给保险证书以代替保险单。空运保险与海运保险十分相似，但总的来说空运保险要便宜得多。

6. Consular invoices are declaration made at the consular of the importing country. They confirm the ex works cost of a consignment.

翻译：领事发票是进口国领事签发的一种申报书，用来证明一批货物的出厂价格。

7. The difference between conciliation and arbitration is that the award of arbitration is final and compulsory whereas opinions of the conciliator are only for the reference of the two sides, and not compulsory.

翻译：调解和仲裁之间的区别在于，仲裁裁决是终结性的，而调解人的建议仅供参考，不具有强制性。

8. One of the parties concerned may refer a dispute to the court which will make a judgment according the law. This is what people call "going through the court". The difference between litigation and arbitration is that the plain-till may take unilateral action without agreement between the two parties in advance.

翻译：诉讼一方的当事人将纠纷提交给法庭，由法庭来依法判决。这就是人们说的打官司。诉讼与仲裁不同之处在于，诉讼的原告可以单方面采取行动，无须双方事先协议。

9. "Sales Contract" 的翻译

全文

合同号：

日期：

订单号：

买方：

卖方：

买卖双方签订本合同并同意按下列条款进行交易：

(1) 品名及规格：

(2) 数量：

(3) 单价：

(4) 金额：

合计

允许溢短装____%

(5) 包装：

(6) 装运口岸：

(7) 目的口岸：

(8) 装船标记：

(9) 装运期限：收到可以转船及分批装运之信用证____天内装出。

(10) 付款条件：开给我方 100%保兑的不可撤回即期付款之信用证，并须注明可在装运日期后 15 天内议付有效。

(11) 保险：按发票 110%保全险及战争险。

由客户自理。

(12) 买方须于____年____月____日前开出本批交易信用证，否则售方有权：不经通知取消本合同，或接受买方对本约未执行的全部或一部分，或对因此遭受的损失提出索赔。

(13) 单据：卖方应向议付银行提供已装船清洁提单、发票、中国商品检验局或工厂出具的品质证明、中国商品检验局出具的数量/重量签订书；如果本合同按 CIF 条件，应再提供可转让的保险单或保险凭证。

(14) 凡以 CIF 条件成交的业务，保额为发票价值的 110%，投保险别以本售货合同中所开列的为限，买方如要求增加保额或保险范围，应于装船前经售方同意，因此而增加的保险费由买方负责。

(15) 质量、数量索赔：如交货质量不符，买方须于货物到达目的港 30 日内提出索赔；数量索赔须于货物到达目的港 15 日内提出。对由于保险公司、船公司和其他转运单位或邮政部门造成的损失卖方不承担责任。

(16) 本合同内所述全部或部分商品，如因人力不可抗拒的原因，以致不能履约或延迟交货，售方概不负责。

(17) 仲裁：凡因执行本合同或与本合同有关事项所发生的一切争执，应由双方通过友好方式协商解决。如果不能取得协议时，则在中国国际经济贸易仲裁委员会根据该仲裁机构的仲裁程序规则进行仲裁。仲裁决定是终局的，对双方具有同等约束力。仲裁费用除非仲裁机构另有决定外，均由败诉一方负担。仲裁也可在双方同意的第三国进行。

(18) 买方在开给售方的信用证上请填注本确认书号码。

(19) 其他条款：

卖方：　　　　　　　　　　　　　　　　　　　　买方：

10. And without the Administration's goal of a "bullet-proof agreement" that business lobbyists can enthusiastically sell to a Republican Congress, the whole process will end up in partisan acrimony that could harm relations with China for years.

翻译：没有商界院外活动集团成员热情地劝说共和党国会采纳政府目标中的防弹性(保护性)协议，那么整个过程将会以党派之间的尖刻的争吵而结束，这会影响以后多年和中国的关系。

11. Also left in the lurch: Wall Street, Hollywood, and Detroit.

这句句子连接上文而说。Leave sb. In the lurch 固定用法，意思是：置某人于困难之中弃之不顾，遗弃某人。完整句型应该是：Wall Street, Hollywood and Detrait are also left in the lurch.

翻译：同样也陷于困境的有华尔街、好莱坞和底特律。

12. Zhu refused to open up much of the lucrative Chinese securities market and insisted on "cultural" restrictions on American movies and music. He also blocked efforts to allow U.S. auto makers to provide fleet financing.

翻译：朱镕基总理不允许开放金融股票市场，坚持对美国电影和音乐作文化方面的限制规定，不让美国汽车商染指投资汽车。

Part 6　词汇及扩展

Notes

sales contract 销售合同
insofar as 在……范围内
bear in mind 记住
terms and conditions 条件(贸易及合同条款的总称)
reconcile…with…使……一致
Ro/ Ro 滚装船，集装箱船的一种，全名为 roll-on / roll-off vessels (ship)
cover note 保险证明书，是保险经纪人签发给保险人的单据，证明已对被保险人的标的物，按照保险证明书上的条款及费率予以保险
bill of lading (B/L) 提单，由船长签发的单据，可确认收到货物，也可作为运输合约代表货物的所有权
to order 凭……指示，以……为抬头
transshipment 转运，转船
alongside blading 备运提单，alongside 指货物未上船，而是在码头待运；blading 是 bill of lading 的简写
be subject to 常遭受……，以……为准
floating policy 流动保险单，按商定费用可按商品的最高价值承保某类货物，不规定转运次数

open cover 预约保险
certificate of value 价值证书
certificate of origin 原产地证明
amicable settlement 友好协商
arbitration 仲裁
conciliation 调解
litigation 诉讼
empirical 经验主义的
allocation 资源配置
consistent 一致的
correlation 相关性
etiquette 礼节，礼仪
protocol 协议
accede 同意，答应
turmoil 骚动，混乱
boycott 联合抵制
attorney 代理人，律师

Part 7　网络学习资源

1. 亚太经合组织是旨在促进自由贸易和经济合作的地区性组织，可见：http://www.apecsec.org.sg。

2. 有关欧盟的贸易其相关信息可见：

http://www.mkaccdb.eu.int

http://www.lib.berkeley.edu/GSSI/eugde.heml

3. 关于产出与贸易增长情况及其对贸易条件的影响，可以在国际货币基金组织、世贸组织、经合组织、世界银行和联合国的网站上查找，其网址分别是：

http://www.imf.org

http://www.wto.org

http://www.oecd.org

http://www.worldbank.org

http://www.un.org/depts/unsd/mbsreg.htm

Unit 3　International Finance 国际金融

Part 1　Intensive Reading　精读

Passage 1　The International Monetary Fund 国际货币基金组织

The International Monetary Fund (IMF) was one of two international institutions established near the end of World War II to ease the transition from a wartime to a peacetime environment and to help prevent the recurrence of the turbulent economic conditions of the Great Depression Era. The IMF was established at the United Nations' Monetary and Financial Conference held at Bretton Wood, New Hampshire, in July 1944. *The main purpose of the IMF is to provide short-term balance-of-payments adjustment loans.*

Today the IMF consists of some 149 countries. The goals of the IMF are to:

(1) Promote international cooperation by providing the means for members to consult on international monetary issues.

(2) Facilitate the growth of international payments.

(3) Promote stability of exchange tares and seek the elimination of exchange restrictions that disrupt international trade.

(4) Make short-term financial resources available to member countries on a temporary basis so as to allow them to correct payment disequilibrium without resorting to measures that would destroy national prosperity.

The IMF can be thought of as a large group of nations that come together and combine resources. Over a given time period, some nations will face balance-of-payment surpluses while others will face deficits. *The IMF can provide assistance by making available international reserves from the surplus nations to countries with temporary payment deficits.* Over the long run, payment deficits must be corrected, and the IMF attempts to ensure that this adjustment will be as prompt and orderly as possible.

The IMF's loanable resources come from two major sources: quotas and loans. Quotas, which are pooled funds of member nations, generate most of the IMF's loanable funds. The size of a member's quota depends on its economic and financial importance in the world. The IMF also obtains loanable resources though loans. Interest and other terms on IMF borrowing arrangements vary considerably. Frequently, interest is charged according to a floating rate and loans are repaid within five to seven years.

Member countries can draw against the IMF's pooled and borrowed funds to finance temporary balance-of-payments deficits. *All IMF loans are subjected to some degree of conditionality. This means that in order to obtain a loan, a deficit nation must agree to implement economic and financial policies as stipulated by the IMF.*

The IMF makes its assistance available through a number of different programs, which vary with international economic conditions. *The IMF generally finances only a part of a member's payment deficits. In addition, IMF assistance is sometimes made in loose connection with World Bank lending, a portion of which can be used for balance-of-payments adjustment loans.*

Passage 2 The International Reserve 国际储备

It is quite natural for a country to have disequilibrium in its international payment. If the country's export exceeds its import, that country enjoys a surplus in the international payments balance, which increases its gold and/ or foreign exchange reserves. However, if the country's imports exceed its exports, then the country will have deficits in its balance of international; payments, which will have to be made up by foreign exchange capital. These foreign exchange capital either comes from its own gold and/ or foreign exchange reserves, or come from foreign borrowings. *The size and terms and conditions of these foreign borrowings depend on the size and scale of the country's own gold and foreign exchange reserves. There are many different forms of these reserves, which are generally called international reserve.*

The international reserve is actually the total amount of a country's international reserve capital, although in different forms, owned by the currency authority of the country, which is usually used for international payments, balancing its overall international payments and maintaining exchange rates of its currency in the international exchange market.

The concept of international reserve can be understood from the following three aspects.

(1) The reserve must be the total foreign exchange capital held by the currency authority of the country, but not the reserve capital by any financial institutions and enterprises.

(2) According to the unified interpretation of the IMF, the international reserve should be composed of four forms.

① Gold reserve.

② Foreign exchange reserve.

③ Reserve position in IMF (General Drawing Rights).

④ Special Drawing Rights.

(3) *The main functions of the international reserve*:

① Intervening the international exchange market to maintain the exchange rate of its currency.
② Balancing short-term disequilibrium of its international payment.
③ Marketing it an important stand-by means of payments in its international trade.
④ Increasing revenue by purchasing foreign state bonds and certificate of deposits.

Passage 3 What Are Futures Markets 什么是期货市场

Futures markets are centralized, regulated markets where an actual commodity is not physically traded; instead, futures contracts are bought and sold. Futures contracts are legally binding agreements and are standardized according to the quality, quantity, delivery time, and location for each commodity. The only variable is price, which is discovered on an exchange trading floor.

Futures prices are quotes for delivering a designated quality and quantity of grain to a specific place and time. The delivery place is established according to the rules of the futures contract. The delivery time consists of certain designated days during the delivery month.

Options on futures, also traded on the floor of a regulated futures exchange, are contracts that convey the right, but not the obligation, to buy or sell a particular futures contract at a certain price for a limited time. Only the seller of the option is obligated to perform. There are two different types of options: calls or puts. A call is an option that gives the buyer the right, but not the obligation, to purchase the underlying futures contract at the strike price on or before the expiration date. A put is an option that gives the seller the right, but not the obligation, to sell the underlying futures contract at the strike price on or before the expiration date.

Passage 4 Hedging: How It Works 套期保值如何运作

The second economic function provided by futures exchanges is price risk management, also known as hedging. Hedging, in its simplest form, is the practice of offsetting the price risk inherent in any cash market position by buying or selling futures contracts.

Hedgers use futures market to protect their businesses from adverse price changes that could negatively impact the bottom-line profitability of their businesses. Hedging can benefit anyone including grain elevator operators, merchandisers, producers, exporters, or processors—who produce, handle, or process any of the agricultural commodities traded on futures exchanges.

Hedging is a two-step process. Depending upon a hedger's cash market situation, the hedger would either buy or sell futures as the first position. Then, at a later date, before the futures hedger would take a second position opposite the opening transaction. The opening and closing positions of the hedge must be for the same commodity number of contracts, and delivery month.

Whether establishing a short or a long hedge, the main objective of hedging is to offset the price risk associated with buying, selling, or holding grain.

Passage 5 What Is a Stock 什么是股票

A share of stock represents ownership in a corporation. A corporation is owned by its stockholders – often thousands of people and institutions – each owing a fraction of the corporation.

When you buy stock in a corporation you become a part-owner or stockholder (also known as shareholder). You immediately own a part, no matter how small, of every building, piece of office furniture, machinery – whatever that company owns.

As a shareholder, you stand to profit when the company profit. You are also legally entitled to say in major policy decisions, such as whether to issue additional stock, sell the company to outside buyers, or change the board of directors. The rule is that each share has the same voting power, so the more share you own, the greater your power.

You can vote in person by attending a corporation's annual meeting. Or you can vote by using an absentee ballot called a proxy, which is mailed before each meeting. The proxy allows a Yes or No vote on a number of proposals. Alternatively, stockholders may authorize their votes to cast consistently with the Board of Directors' recommendations.

Part 2 Extensive Reading 泛读

Passage 1 Balance of Payments 国际收支

The Balance of Payments (BOP) is the method countries use to monitor all international monetary transactions at a specific period of time. *The Balance of Payments (BOP) is a statistical statement that summarizes, for a specific period (typically a year or quarter), the economic transactions of an economy with the rest of the world.*

During the course of a year the residents of one country engage in a vast number and variety of transactions with residents of other countries — exports and imports of merchandise and services, cash payments and receipts, gold floes, gifts, loans and investments, and other transaction. These transactions are interrelated in many ways, and together they comprise the international trade and payments of the national economy.

As a statistical classification and summary of all economic transactions between domestic and foreign residents over a stipulated period (ordinarily one year), the Balance of Payments of a nation affords an overall view of its international economic position. For this reason, the Balance of Payment is particularly helpful to government authorities—treasuries and central banks —

who are directly charged with the responsibility of maintaining external economic stability. Moreover, international trade is so important to many countries that the Balance of Payments must be carefully considered in the formulation of domestic economic policies, such as employment, wages, and investment.

The Balance of Payments of a country may also influence the decisions of business people. The experienced international trader on investor does not overlook the intimate bearing of the Balance of Payments upon the foreign exchange market and the course of government policy. A domestic exporter may hesitate to deal with an importer if it is suspected that the authorities of the importer's country will shortly impose or tighten exchange controls in the face of an adverse Balance of Payments. Dealers in foreign exchange also pay close attention to the Balance of Payments of countries whose currencies they handle in daily transactions. Failure to realize the close dependence of international business upon the Balance of Payments of the domestic and foreign countries has often led to losses or even outright business failures.

Three principles underlying the compilation of the Balance of Payments of a nation are worth special emphasis. First, only economic transactions between domestic and foreign residents are entered in the Balance of Payments. Second, a distinction is made between debit and credit transactions. Third, the Balance of Payments is a double-entry accounting statement.

1. The Concept of Residence

The Balance of Payments summarizes all economic transactions between domestic and foreign residents. Residence should not be confused with the legal notion of citizenship or nationality.

Individuals, who represent their government in foreign countries, including members of the armed forces, are always considered residents of their own country. Thus, when a member of the American armed forces buys a glass of wine in France, an international transaction occurs that enters the Balance of Payments of both the United State and France. Individuals who do not represent a government are considered to be residents of that country in which they have a permanent residence.

In preparing a Balance of Payments, the question of individual residence is much less important than the question of business residence. A corporation is a resident of the country in which it is incorporated, but its foreign branches and subsidiaries are viewed as foreign residents. Hence, shipments between and American concern and its oversea branch are international transactions and as such, are entered in the U.S. Balance of Payments.

2. International Transactions as Debits and Credits

Transactions between domestic and foreign residents are entered in the Balance of Payments either as debits or credits. Debit transactions are all transactions that involve payments by domestic residents to foreign residents. Credit transactions are all transactions that involve receipts domestic residents from foreign residents.

This distinction is most clearly seen when we examine transactions between American and foreign residents and assume that all payments and receipts are made in dollars. Then debit transactions involve dollar payments by Americans to foreigner, and credit transactions involve dollar receipts by Americans from foreigners.

Double-Entry Accounting. Although it is convenient to speak of "debit transactions" and "credit transactions", each international transaction is an exchange of assets and therefore has both a debit and a credit side. Conceptually, therefore, the Balance of Payments is a double-entry accounting statement in which total debits and credits are always equal. We can demonstrate this double-entry approach with some hypothetical examples.

3. Balance of Payments of Country X

Table 3-1 depicts the Balance of Payments for a fictitious country X.

Table 3-1 The Balance of Payments for a Fictitious Country X

(million dollars)

	Debits	Credits
A. Current Account		
1. Merchandise exports		600
2. Merchandise imports	500	
3. Service	75	100
Net goods and service balance		125
4. Unilateral transfers		
To abroad	100	
From abroad		25
Net current account balance		50
B. Capital Account		
5. Direct investment		
To abroad		60
From abroad		30
6. Portfolio investment		
To abroad		20
From abroad		40

	cont
7. Short-term capital (net)	
To abroad	150
From abroad	30
Net capital account balance	130
C. Official Reserves Account	
8. Gold export or import (net)	10
9. Decrease or increase in foreign exchange (net)	60
10. Increase or decrease in liabilities to foreign central banks (net)	20
Net official reserves account balance	90
11. Net errors and omissions	10

4. Content of BOP

All trades conducted by both the private and public sectors are accounted for in the BOP in order to determine how much money is going in and out of a country. It covers:

① all the goods, services, factor income and current transfers an economy receives from or provides to the rest of the world.

② capital transfers and changes in an economy's external financial claims and liabilities.

Transactions are generally between residents and non-residents. The exceptions are the exchange of transferable foreign financial assets between residents and transferable foreign financial liabilities between non-residents. For the purposes of the Balance of Payments, residency relates to the economic territory of a country, not nationality. An international unit is resident unit when it has a center of economic interest in the economic territory of a country.

The Balance of Payments methodology uses a double-entry accounting system. This means that every recorded item should have a credit and a debit. If a country has received money, this is known as a credit, and, if a country has paid or given money, the transaction is counted as a debit. Theoretically, the BOP should be zero, meaning that assets (credits) and liabilities (debits) should balance. Summarized in Table 3-2.

Table 3-2 Balance of Payments Credit and Debit

Credit	Debit
Exports of goods and services	Imports of goods and services
Income receivable from abroad	Income payable abroad
Transfers from abroad	Transfers to abroad
Increases in external liabilities	Decreases in external liabilities
Decreases in external assets	Increases in external assets

In practice, the figures rarely balance to the point where they cancel each other out. This is the result of errors or omissions in the compilation of statements. A separate balancing item is used to offset the credit or debit.

The BOP is divided into three main categories: the current account, the capital account and the financial account. Within these three categories are sub-divisions, each of which accounts for a different type of international monetary transaction.

(1) he Current Account

The current account is used to mark the inflow and outflow of goods and services into a country. Earnings on investments, both public and private, are also put into the current account. The current account consists of international dealings in goods (visible trade) and services (invisible trade). Invisible trade includes payments for overseas embassies and military bases: interest, profit and dividends from overseas investment; earnings from tourism and transportation.

Within the current account are credits and debits on the trade of merchandise, which includes goods such as raw materials and manufactured goods that are bought, sold or given away (possibly in the form of aid). Services refer to receipts from tourism, transportation (like the levy that must be paid in Egypt when a ship passes through the Suez Canal), engineering, business service fees (from lawyers or management consulting, for example), and royalties from patents and copyrights. When combined, goods and services together make up a country's Balance of Trade (BOT). The BOT is typically the biggest bulk of a country's Balance of Payments as it makes up total imports and exports. If a country has a Balance of Trade deficit, it imports more than it exports, and if it has a Balance of Trade surplus, it exports more than it imports.

Receipts from income-generating assets such as stocks (in the form of dividends) are also recorded in the current account. The last component of the current account is unilateral transfers. These are credits that are mostly worker's remittances, which are salaries sent back into the home country of a national working abroad, as well as foreign aid that is directly received.

(2) The Capital Account

The capital account is where all international capital transfers are recorded. This refers to the acquisition or disposal of non-financial assets (for example, a physical asset such as land) and non-produced assets, which are needed for production but have not been produced, like a mine used for the extraction of diamonds.

The capital account is broken down into the monetary flows branching from debt forgiveness, the transfer of goods, and financial assets by migrants leaving or entering a country, the transfer of ownership on fixed assets (assets such as equipment used in the production process to generate income), the transfer of funds received to the sale or acquisition of fixed assets, gift and inheritance taxes, death levies, and, finally, uninsured damage to fixed assets.

(3) The Financial Account

In the financial account, international monetary flows related to investment in business, real estate, bonds and stocks are documented.

Also included are government-owned assets such as foreign reserves, gold, special drawing rights (SDRs) held with the International Monetary Fund, private assets held abroad, and direct foreign investment. Assets owned by foreigners, private and official, are also recorded in the financial account.

5. The Balancing Act

The current account should be balanced against the combined-capital and financial accounts. However, as mentioned above, this rarely happens. We should also note that, with fluctuating exchange rates, the change in the value of money can add to BOP discrepancies. When there is a deficit in the current account, which is a balance of trade deficit, the difference can be borrowed or funded by the capital account. If a country has a fixed asset abroad, this borrowed amount is marked as a capital account outflow. However, the sale of that fixed asset would be considered a current account inflow (earnings from investments). The current account deficit would thus be funded.

When a country has a current account deficit that is financed by the capital account, the country is actually foregoing capital assets for more goods and services. If a country is borrowing money to fund its current account deficit, this would appear as an inflow of foreign capital in the BOP.

6. Liberalizing the Accounts

The rise of global financial transactions and trade in the late-20th century spurred BOP and macroeconomic liberalization in many developing nations. With the advent of the emerging market economic boom—in which capital flows into these markets tripled from USD 50 million to USD 150 million from the late 1980s until the Asian crisis—developing countries were urged to lift restrictions on capital and financial-account transactions in order to take advantage of these capital inflows. Many of these countries had restrictive macroeconomic policies, by which regulations prevented foreign ownership of financial and non-financial assets. The regulations also limited the transfer of funds abroad. But with capital and financial account liberalization, capital markets began to grow, not only allowing a more transparent and sophisticated market for investors, but also giving rise to foreign direct investment. For example, investments in the form of a new power station would bring a country greater exposure to new technologies and efficiency, eventually increasing the nation's overall gross domestic product by allowing for greater volumes of production. Liberalization can also facilitate less risk by allowing greater diversification in various markets.

Passage 2　Foreign Exchange Market 国际外汇市场

1. The Concept of the Foreign-Exchange Market

The foreign-exchange market refers to the organizational setting within which individuals, businesses, governments, and banks buy and sell foreign currencies and other debt instruments. Only a small fraction of daily transactions in foreign exchange actually involve trading of currency. Most foreign-exchange transactions involve the transfer of bank deposits. Major U.S. banks, such as Citibank, maintain inventories of foreign exchange in the form of foreign-denominated deposits held in branch or correspondent banks in foreign cities. Americans can obtain this foreign exchange from hometown banks that, in turn, purchase it from Citibank.

The foreign-exchange market is by far the largest and most liquid market in the world. The estimated worldwide amount of foreign-exchange transactions is around $1.5 trillion a day. Individual trades of $200 million to $500 million are not uncommon. Quoted prices change as often as 20 times a minute. It has been estimated that the world's most active exchange rates can change up to 18,000 times during a single day.

Not all currencies are traded on foreign-exchange markets. Currencies that are not traded are avoided for reasons ranging from political instability to economic uncertainty. Sometimes a country's currency is not exchanged for the simple reason that the country produces very few products of interest to other countries.

Unlike stock or commodity exchanges, the foreign-exchange market is not an organized struc-ture. It has no centralized meeting place and no formal requirements for participation. Nor is the foreign-exchange market limited to any one country. For any currency, such as the U.S. dollar, the foreign-exchange market consists of all locations where dollars are exchanged for other national currencies. Three of the largest foreign-exchange markets in the world are located in London, New York, and Tokyo. A dozen or so other market centers also exist around the world, such as Paris and Zurich. Because foreign-exchange dealers are in constant telephone and computer contact, the market is very competitive; in effect, it functions no differently than if it were a centralized market.

The foreign-exchange market opens on Monday morning in Hong Kong, which is still Sunday evening in New York. As the day progresses, markets open in Tokyo, Frankfurt, London, New York, Chicago, San Francisco, and elsewhere. As the West Coast markets of the United

States close, Hong Kong is only one hour away from opening for Tuesday business. Indeed, the foreign-exchange market is a round-the-clock operation. A typical foreign-exchange market functions at three levels.

① In transactions between comercial banks and their commercial customers, who are the ultimate demanders and suppliers of foreign exchange.

② In the domestic interbank market conducted through brokers.

③ In active trading in foreign exchange with banks overseas.

Exporters, importers, investors, and tourists buy and sell foreign exchange from and to commercial banks rather than each other. As an example, consider the import of German autos by a U.S. dealer. The dealer is billed for each car it imports at the rate of 50,000 euros per car. The U.S. dealer cannot write a check for this amount because it does not have a checking account denominated in euros. Instead, the dealer goes to the foreign-exchange department of, say, Chase Manhattan Bank to arrange payment. If the exchange rate is 1.1 euros = $1, the auto dealer writes a check to Chase Manhattan Bank for $45,454.55 (50,000/1.1 = 45,454.55) per car. Chase Manhattan will then pay the German manufacturer 50,000 euros per car in Germany. Chase Manhattan is able to do this because it has a checking deposit in euros at its branch in Bonn.

The major banks who trade foreign exchange generally do not deal directly with one another but instead use the services of foreign-exchange brokers. The purpose of a broker is to permit the trading banks to maintain desired foreign-exchange balances. If at a particular moment a bank does not have the proper foreign-exchange balances, it can turn to a broker to buy additional foreign currency or sell the surplus. Brokers thus provide a wholesale, interbank market in which trading banks can buy and sell foreign exchange. Brokers are paid a commission for their services by the selling bank.

The third tier of the foreign-exchange market consists of the transactions between the trading banks and their overseas branches or foreign correspondents. Although several dozen U.S. banks trade in foreign exchange, it is the major New York banks that usually carry out transactions with foreign banks. The other, inland trading banks meet their foreign-exchange needs by maintaining correspondent relationships with New York banks. Trading with foreign banks permits the matching of supply and demand of foreign exchange in the New York market. These international transactions are carried out primarily by telephone and computers.

2. The Types of Foreign Exchange Market: Foreign Bank –Note Market

The earliest experience that many of us have of dealing with foreign currency is on our first overseas vacation. When not traveling abroad, most of us have very little to do with foreign exchange, which is not used in the course of ordinary commerce, espe cially in the United States. The foreign exchange with which we deal when on vacation involves bank notes and, quite frequently, foreign-currency-denominated traveler's checks.

Our experience changing currencies on vacation should not lead us to believe that large-scale international financial transactions encounter similar costs. The bank-note market used by travelers involves large spreads because generally only small amounts are traded, which nevertheless require as much paperwork as bigger commercial trades. Another reason why the spreads are large is that each bank and currency exchange must hold many different currencies to be able to provide cus tomers with what they want, and these notes do not earn interest. This involves an opportunity, or inventory, cost, as well as some risk from short-term changes in exchange rates. Furthermore, bank robbers, in which the United States does not have a monopoly, specialize in bank notes; therefore, those who hold large amounts of them are forced to take security precautions, especially when moving bank notes from branch to branch or country to country. A further risk faced in the exchange of bank notes is the acceptance of counterfeit bills, which frequently show up in for eign financial centers. It is worth noting that because banks face a lower risk of theft of traveler's checks and because the companies that issue them American Express, VISA, Thomas Cook, MasterCard, and so on will quickly credit the banks that accept their checks, many banks give a more favorable buyer exchange rate on checks than on bank notes. Furthermore, issuers of traveler's checks enjoy the use of the money paid for the checks before they are cashed, and the banks selling the checks to customers do not face an inventory cost; payment to a check issuer by a check-selling bank is made only after checks have been purchased by a customer. The benefits to the issuers and sellers of traveler's checks keep down the spread.

While the exchange of bank notes between ordinary private customers and banks takes place in the retail market, banks trade their surpluses of notes between themselves in the wholesale market. The wholesale market involves firms which specialize in buying and selling foreign bank notes with commercial banks and currency exchanges. These currency-trading firms are bank-note wholesalers.

As an example of the workings of the wholesale market, during the summer a British bank might receive large numbers of Deutschemarks from Germans traveling in Britain. The same British bank may also be selling large numbers of Italian lire to British tourists leaving for vacations in Italy. The British bank will sell its surplus Deutschemarks to a bank-note wholesaler in London, who might then transport the mark notes back to Germany or to a nonGerman bank in need of mark notes. The British bank will buy lire from a wholesaler, who may well have transported the lire from Italy or else bought them from banks which had purchased lire from vacationing Italians. The spreads on the wholesale level are less than retail bank-note spreads, generally well below 2 percent, because larger amounts are generally traded.

3. The Types of Foreign Exchange Market: The Spot Foreign Exchange Market

Far larger than the bank-note market is the spot foreign exchange market, which is involved with the exchange of currencies held in different currency-denominated bank accounts. The spot exchange rate, which is determined in the spot market, is of the speed of communications, significant events have virtually instantaneous impacts everywhere in the world despite the huge distances separating market par ticipants. This is what makes the foreign exchange market just as efficient as a con ventional stock or commodity market housed under a single roof.

The efficiency of the spot foreign exchange market is revealed in the extremely narrow spreads between buying and selling prices. These spreads can be smaller than a tenth of a percent of the value of currency exchanged and are therefore about one-fiftieth or less of the spread faced on bank notes by international travelers. The effi ciency of the market is also manifest in the electrifying speed with which exchange rates respond to the continuous flow of information that bombards the market. Par ticipants cannot afford to miss a beat in the frantic pulse of this dynamic, global market. Indeed, the bankers and brokers that constitute the foreign exchange market can scarcely detach themselves from the video monitors that provide the latest news and prices as fast as the information can travel along the telephone wires and radio waves of business news wire services such as Dow Jones Telerate and Reuters.

In the United States, as in most other markets, there are two levels on which the foreign exchange market operates a direct interbank level and an indirect level via brokers. In the case of interbank trading, banks trade directly with each other, and all participating banks are market-makers. That is, in the direct interbank mar ket, banks quote buying and selling prices to each other. This is known as an open-bid double auction. Because there is no central location of the market and because trading is continuous, the direct market can be characterized as a decentralized, continuous, open-bid, double-auction market.

In the case of foreign exchange brokers, of which there were 16 versus over 150 commercial banks in the New York market in 1994, so-called limit orders are placed with brokers by banks. For example, a commercial bank will place an order with a broker to purchase £10 million at \$1.5550/£. The broker puts this on the "books" and attempts to match the purchase order with sell orders for pounds from other banks. While the market-making banks take positions on their own behalves and for customers, brokers deal only for others, showing callers their best rates, called their inside spread, and charging a commission to both buying and selling banks. Because of its structure, the indirect broker-based market can be characterized as a quasi-centralized, continuous, limit-book, single-auction market.

In the direct interbank market, which is the largest part of the foreign exchange market, bankers call foreign exchange dealers at other banks and "ask for the market". The caller does not say whether he or she wants to buy or to sell, nor does the caller state the amount to be traded. The caller might say, "Your market in sterling, please." This means, "At what price are you willing to buy and at what price are you willing to sell British pounds for U.S. dollars?" (British pounds are called sterling.) In replying, a foreign exchange dealer must attempt to determine whether the caller really wants to buy or to sell and must relate this to what his or her own preferred position is. This is a subtle and tricky game involving human judgment. Bluff and counterbluff are used. A good trader, with a substantial order in pounds, may first ask for the market in Canadian dollars. After placing an order he or she might say, "By the way, what's your market in (British) sterling?" Dealers sometimes have their assistants place really large orders, in an effort to obtain favorable quotes: anticipation of a very large order might cause a quoting bank to increase its spread. A difference in quotation that shows up in the fourth decimal place can mean thousands of dollars on a large order. It is rather like poker, with massive stakes.

If a banker who has been called wants to sell pounds, he or she will quote on the side that is felt to be cheap for pounds, given this banker's feel of the market. For example, if the banker believes that other banks are selling pounds at $1.6120/£, he or she might quote $1.6118/£ as the selling price, along with a buying price that is also correspondingly low. Having considered the two-way price, the caller will state whether he or she wishes to buy or sell, and the amount. Once the rate has been quoted, it must be honored whatever the decision of the caller, up to a predetermined limit set by convention among market makers. The caller has only seconds to decide. Good judgment of the counterparty and good judgment of the direction of the market are essential in this multibillion-dollar game. It is important to be accurate and constantly in touch with events.

Passage 3　The World Bank 世界银行

The "World Bank" is the International Bank for Reconstruction and Development (IBRD). It was organized in 1949 along with the IMF to aid in rebuilding the world economy. *It is owned by the governments of 151 countries in the world, and its capital is subscribed by those governments. It provides funds to borrowers by borrowing funds in the world capital markets and from the proceeds of loan repayments as well as retained earnings.* At its founding, the bank's major objective was to serve as an international financing facility to function in reconstruction and development. With the Marshall Plan providing the impetus for European reconstruction, the bank was able to turn its efforts toward the developing countries.

Generally, IBRD lends money to a government for the purpose of developing the country's economic infrastructure, such as road, sewage treatment system, and power generating facilities. Funds are directed towards developing countries at more advanced stages of economic and social growth. Funds are lent only to members of the IMF, usually when private capital is unavailable at reasonable terms. Loans generally have a grace period of five years and are repayable over a period of up to fifteen years.

The projects receiving IBRD assistance usually require the importing of heavy industrial equipment, thus providing an export market for many U.S. goods. Generally, bank loans are made to cover only import needs. They are issued in foreign convertible currencies and must be repaid in those currencies at long-term rates.

The World Bank has several special operational emphases, including environmental and women's issues. *Given that the Bank's primary mission is to support the quality of life of people in developing member countries, it is easy to see why environmental and women's issues are receiving increasing attention.* On the environmental side, the Bank is concerned that its development funds are being used by the recipient countries in an environmentally responsible way. Internal concerns, as well as pressure by external groups, have led to the continuance of significant research and environmental projects.

The women's issues category, specially known as Women in Development (WID), is part of a larger emphasis on human resources. The importance of improving human capital and the welfare of families is perceived as a key aspect of development. The WID initiative was established in 1988, and it is oriented to increase women's productivity and income. Bank lending for women's issues is most pronounced education, population, health, nutrition and agriculture.

Passage 4   Stock Prices 股票价格

A stock does not have a fixed, objective worth. At any moment, it's only as valuable as people think it is.

When you buy a stock, you're making a bet that a lot of other people are going to want to buy that stock, too – and that the price will go up as a result. Your bet is gamble – but it's not like playing roulette, where the ball may land on 11 even if everyone in the room has bet on 23.

In the stock market, the betting itself influences the outcome. If many investors bet on ABC stock, the price of ABC stock will rise. It will become a more valuable stock – simply because a number of people thought it would. When you are trading stock, then, you have to keep one eye on the other traders to see how they are betting.

The stock market is, however, more than a lot of invertors watching what other investors do. They also watch the companies very carefully. Since the value of share is directly related to how well the company is doing, investors naturally look for the companies with the best prospects for strong, sustained earning.

How do you judge a company's prospects? By current or anticipated earnings, the desirability of its product or service, competition, availability of new markets, management strengths and many other consideration. These are the factors that stock analysts track in trying to predict whether a stock's value will rise or fall.

Part 3   Academic Reading   学术阅读

Passage   Global Financial Stability Still at Risk 全球金融稳定依然面临风险

Nearly four years after the onset of the largest financial crisis since the Great Depression, global financial stability is still not assured and significant policy challenges remain to be addressed. Balance sheet restructuring is incomplete and proceeding slowly, and leverage is still high. The interaction between banking and sovereign credit risks in the euro area remains a critical factor, and policies are needed to tackle fiscal and banking sector vulnerabilities. At the global level, regulatory reforms are still required to put the financial sector on a sounder footing. At the same time, accommodative policies in advanced economies and relatively favorable fundamentals in some emerging market countries are spurring capital inflows. This means that policymakers in emerging market countries will need to watch diligently for signs of asset price bubbles and excessive credit.

Even though global economic growth has accelerated somewhat, global financial stability has yet to be secured. The two-track global recovery—with advanced countries growing much more slowly than the rest of the world— continues to pose policy challenges. The slow growth prospects of advanced economies and the continued weakness in their fiscal balances have raised the market's sensitivity to debt sustainability risks. The evident links between weak balance sheets of government and banking sectors have led to renewed pressures in funding markets in the euro area and widening strains. At the same time, accommodative monetary policies in advanced countries and relatively favorable fundamentals in emerging market economies have spurred capital flows to such economies. This creates upward pressure on asset markets in receiving countries, while raising the latent risk that inflows could reverse and, as a result, poses considerable policy challenges on how best to absorb the flows.

Notwithstanding these factors, financial market performance has been favorable thus far in early 2011, reflecting the more positive economic climate, ample liquidity, and expanding risk appetite. Equity markets in advanced and emerging market countries have risen since the October 2010 *Global Financial Stability Report* (GFSR). Commodity prices have taken off while oil, food, metals, and raw material prices all rising rapidly. However, such positive developments have been notably absent for many advanced country sovereigns and their banking systems (Figure 3.1). In fact, there are now several cases in which sovereign credit default swap (CDS) spreads exceed those in large emerging market countries. Banks in those advanced economies also have elevated CDS spreads.

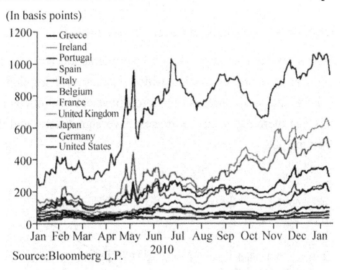

Figure 3.1 Sovereign Credit Default Swap Spreads

1. Interaction between Sovereign and Banking Sector Risks Has Intensified

Despite improvements in market conditions since the October 2010 GFSR, sovereign risks within the euro area have on balance intensified and spilled over to more countries. Government bond spreads in some cases reached highs that were significantly above the levels seen during the turmoil last May. Pressures on Ireland were particularly severe and led to an EU-ECB-IMF program. Correlations between the average sovereign yields of Greece and Ireland and the yields of Portugal have remained high, but correlations have increased sharply in recent months with the yields of Spain, and to a lesser extent, Italy, as the tensions spread (Figure 3.2).

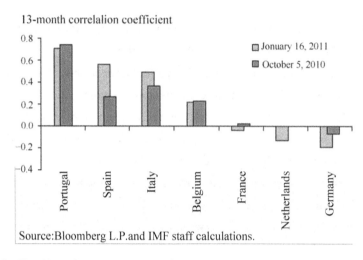

Figure 3.2   Ten-Year Government Bond Correlation with Average of Greece and Ireland

While still contained to the euro area, the adverse interaction between the sovereign and banking risks in a number of countries has intensified, leading to disruptions in some funding markets. Figure 3.3 shows that CDS spreads written on financial institutions have increased the most in countries in which there has been the greatest sovereign stress—and this relationship is more positive now than in 2008.

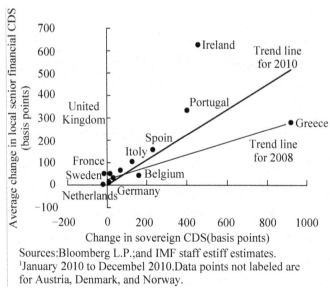

Figure 3.3   Sovereign and Bank Credit Default Swap Spreads[1]

Smaller and more domestically-focused banks in some countries have found access to private wholesale funding sources curtailed. Many banks that have retained access have faced higher costs and are only able to borrow at very short maturities.

Several countries, as well as their main banks, face substantial financing needs in 2011 as bank and sovereign debt-to-GDP ratios have risen substantially in the last several years (see IMF Fiscal Monitor Update and Figure 3.4). The confluence of funding pressures and continued banking sector vulnerabilities leaves financial systems fragile and highly vulnerable to deterioration in market sentiment.

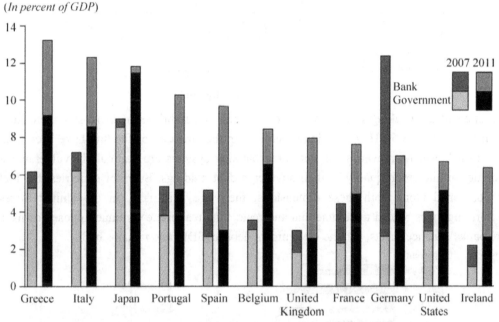

Sources:Dealogic; IMF, World 500nomic Outlook database; and IMF staff calculations.
Note: The first Slacked bar for each counlry is for bonds that were due in 2007 and the second stacked bar is for bonds due in 20011. In order to compare current funding needs with the past the dataset only includes a subset of total bonds due and so does not r eflect total funding needs. The chart also does not include interest payments.

Figure 3.4 Government and Bank Bonds Due

2. Little Progress on Deleveraging

The build-up of gross debt accumulated by the private sector in a number of advanced markets has in most cases been only partly reversed, if at all (Figure 3.5).

Private sector debt-to-GDP ratios should fall gradually over time as economic activity picks up, but the high current debt levels and the usual tendency for loan losses to lag the recovery could still pose risks to the banking system.

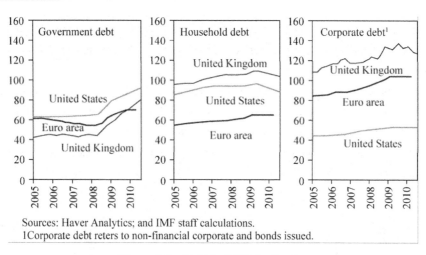

Figure 3.5　Debt to GDP, by Sector

Most countries' banking systems have reduced their vulnerabilities by increasing their Tier 1 capital ratios (Figure 3.6). However, improvements in the structure of funding have been more difficult to achieve. Moreover, some euro-area banking systems are particularly vulnerable to deterioration in the credit quality of their sovereign debt holdings. Even for countries that look better positioned along both these dimensions, there are still risks. In the United States, nonperforming loans related to commercial and residential real estate continue to pose downside risks to banks' balance sheets, and the government debt-to-GDP ratio remains high.

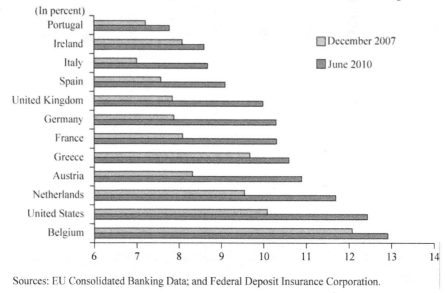

Figure 3.6　Banking System Tier 1 Capital Ratios

Still-high levels of private debt in some countries are likely to dampen both private sector demand for credit and banks' willingness to lend, weighing on the economic recovery. Although accommodative monetary policies are appropriate to help spur recovery, low interest rates and the use of quantitative easing can have adverse financial stability side effects, including by encouraging riskier investments. Low rates also pose a challenge for fixed-income investors such as pension funds and insurance companies that rely on higher-yielding assets to match their long-term fixed liabilities.

3. Resurgent Capital Flows to Emerging Market Economies

Stronger economic fundamentals in some key emerging markets, along with low interest rates in advanced countries, have led to a rebound in capital flows, after the significant drop at the height of the financial crisis. Net inflows to emerging market countries now represent around 4 percent of GDP in aggregate (Figure 3.7). By comparison, inflows prior to the crisis were above 6 percent of GDP. Capital inflows have been accompanied by a large increase in equity and bond issuance, potentially limiting some of their effects on the price of these assets.

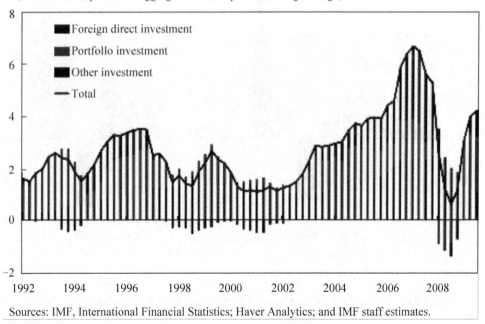

Figure 3.7 Capital Flows to Emerging Markets

These capital flows may be partly driven by structural factors underlying changes in asset allocation decisions by institutional investors who are now looking at emerging market assets more favorably. However, these flows are also being driven by carry trades, in which investors hope to profit from interest rate differentials and expectations of exchange rate appreciation. Such expectations often accompany policies designed to temporarily limit exchange rate appreciation. Forward interest rates show that the current differential between emerging and advanced country policy rates is expected to rise, which will further increase the incentive for such carry trades. This suggests a vulnerability to reversals in response to, for instance, an unexpected rise in advanced country interest rates, a shift in growth prospects in emerging market countries, or a rise in risk aversion.

Capital inflows are normally beneficial for recipient countries, but sustained capital inflows can strain the absorptive capacity of local financial systems. Retail flows into debt and equity mutual funds have been strong, particularly for equity funds, and could give rise to the formation of asset price bubbles if local assets are in limited supply (Figure 3.8).

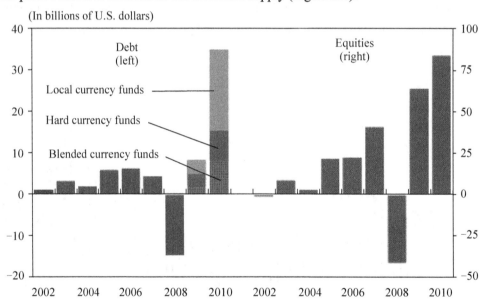

Sources: EPFR; and IMF, staff estimates.

Figure 3.8　Annual Retail Flows to Emerging Market Debt and Epuity Mutual Funds

Although most measures of equity valuations are within historical ranges, "hot spots" appear to be emerging in the equity markets in Colombia and Mexico and, to a lesser extent, in India and Peru.

Inflows can also lead to a rapid increase in private sector indebtedness in recipient countries. As shown in Figure 3.9, in some economies in Asia and Latin America, nonfinancial private debt is approaching the maximum ratios reached between 1996 and 2010 (Brazil, Chile, China, India, and Korea, for example).(*Private sector debt includes domestic and cross-border bank credit, and domestic and international corporate debt*). While in some countries the change may represent financial deepening and healthy market development, in other countries it could signal an increase in risk, and it is important that country authorities remain vigilant.

A further symptom of large capital inflows is that lower-rated entities gain greater market access to issue debt, lowering the average quality of assets held by investors. There has been an increase in the proportion of debt issued by lower-grade credits during the last two years.

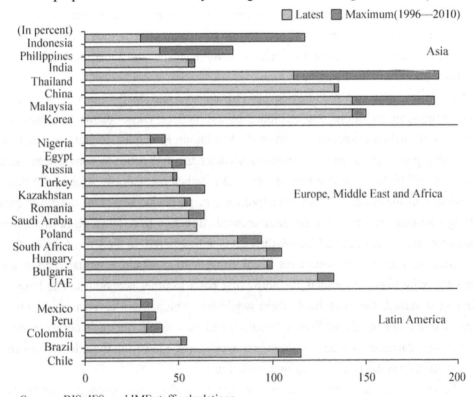

Sources: BIS; IFS; and IMF staff calculations.

Figure 3.9 Non-Financial Private Sector Debt to GDP

4. Policy Priorities

Policy action is needed to ensure that the required restructuring and balance sheet repair take place—both for banks and sovereigns— and that regulatory reforms move forward.

The time purchased with the extraordinary support measures of the past few years is running out. Low policy interest rates that are close to the zero bound are likely to have a diminishing effect over time. Fiscal stimulus and further government support of the financial sector are also becoming increasingly unpalatable politically. It is clear that monetary and fiscal policy support can be helpful in the short term, but that such support is no substitute for structural solutions to longstanding problems. Such solutions need to address sovereign risk and financial fragilities in a holistic and comprehensive fashion.

5. Breaking the Adverse Sovereign-Financial Loop

The root of the problem in many of the countries hit by the crisis—the detrimental interaction between sovereign and financial sector risk—must be addressed. This applies in particular to the euro- area countries where, despite the set-up of area-wide instruments, markets remain concerned about the lack of a sufficiently comprehensive and consistent strategy to repair fiscal balance sheets and the financial system.

All countries with outsized debt levels—inside and outside the euro area—must make further medium-term, ambitious, and credible progress on fiscal consolidation strategies, together with better public debt management based on the Stockholm Principles. In particular, in countries facing funding pressures, there is a continued need for the authorities to convince markets that they can, and will, reduce reliance on rollovers and lengthen the maturity structure of their debt. This process will inevitably involve other policies, in particular structural measures aimed at supporting potential growth. Solid movements in this direction have taken place in a number of euro- area countries, but sustained follow-through is still required. In the United States, the delay of a credible strategy for medium-term fiscal consolidation would eventually drive up U.S. interest rates, with knock-on effects for borrowing costs in other economies. The longer fiscal stabilization is stalled, the more likely there would be a sharper rise in Treasury yields, which could prove disruptive for global financial markets and the world economy. Another country with high debt levels, Japan, also needs to continue to work toward lowering those levels and ensuring fiscal sustainability in the face of an aging population.

At the same time, financial system repair must be undertaken—strengthening the banking sector through well-targeted remedial actions, removing the tail risks, and establishing a better regulatory system.

In the European Union, the steps listed below are needed to reduce uncertainty and help restore confidence in markets.

① Further rigorous and credible bank stress testing is required along with time-bound follow-up plans for recapitalization and restructuring of viable, undercapitalized institutions and closure of nonviable ones.

② The effective size of the European Financial Stability Facility should be increased and it should have a more flexible mandate. For countries where the banking system represents a large proportion of the economy, it is now even more essential to ensure access to sufficient funds, going beyond national backstops whenever necessary.

③ Euro area-wide resolution mechanisms need to be deployed and strengthened as needed. The introduction of a pan-European bank resolution framework with an EU-wide fiscal backstop would help decouple sovereign and banking risks.

④ The European Central Bank will need to continue to supply liquidity to banks that need it and keep its Securities Markets Program active, while also recognizing that this is a temporary set of measures and will not solve the underlying problems.

In the United States, efforts are needed to address the headwinds from the still-damaged real estate markets.

① It is important to find ways to mitigate the negative macro-financial linkages from the large "shadow inventory" of houses for sale (i.e., properties that are already in foreclosure or expected to default) that is likely to dampen house prices for some time to come and exacerbate negative home equity problems. Steps are also needed to revive securitization markets, while at the same time making sure that structured credit products are consistent with systemic stability.

② As emphasized in the conclusions of the recent Financial Sector Assessment Program, an overhaul is needed of the U.S. housing finance system, including the role of the mortgage-related, government-sponsored enterprises. These could be either privatized or converted to public utilities with an explicit (and explicitly funded) guarantee. The authorities should not delay efforts to create an action plan for the future.

In many advanced countries, bank balance sheet and operational restructuring is necessary to preserve the long-term viability of financial institutions and hence reduce the implicit pressure on the sovereign balance sheet in these countries. In some banking systems, the problems are less cyclical and more structural in nature—namely chronically low profitability and fading business lines. Where durable solutions are not possible, effective resolution tools are required that can, in an increasingly complex and interconnected global financial system, preserve financial stability, while ultimately allowing losses to be borne by creditors rather than taxpayers. Governments need to consider carefully how, through better capital structures and possibly through restrictions on the scope and riskiness of activities, large financial institutions can be less of a threat to overall systemic stability and to sovereign balance sheets.

6. Regulatory Reform Efforts Need to Continue

At the global level, regulatory reform efforts have been moving forward, but increasingly suffer from a combination of fatigue and the sheer complexity of the issues. Progress has been made on micro-prudential banking regulation aimed at ensuring the solidity of individual institutions, though important gaps remain. Macro-prudential policymaking, which aims to preserve the stability of the financial system as a whole, is still in its infancy in most countries, and there are concerns that systemic vulnerabilities may build up again before solid progress is made to prevent such a build-up. Financial systems will need to adjust to the new reforms, including as the recovery takes hold and interest rates rise. This will be more challenging for those countries, such as Japan, that have had low interest rates and a build-up of debt over a long period of time.

New entities are being established to improve systemic oversight. They should waste no time in collecting and analyzing data and issuing policy advice, especially in light of the present low interest rate environment that could well be laying the ground for new financial vulnerabilities. The new European Systemic Risk Board has become operational this month, and markets will watch closely for strong risk warnings and recommendations. The new Financial Stability Oversight Council in the United States, which has already initiated regular meetings, needs to demonstrate that the financial stability arrangements and surrounding regulatory structure have been upgraded in light of the lessons from the crisis.

Guidelines to identify systemically-important financial institutions and measure their contribution to systemic risk are being worked out, though how to mitigate the risks they pose to the financial system is still an open question.

Particularly, how to deal with systemically important nonbanks and markets is a difficult and outstanding issue. Moreover, methods to improve the quality of supervision and produce a fully functional cross-border resolution scheme are still on the "to do" list.

7. Coping with Capital Inflows

The need for macro-prudential policymaking is also very relevant for emerging market economies facing absorptive constraints on capital inflows. These policies are complements, not substitutes, for traditional macroeconomic policies. So far, evidence of asset price bubbles and credit booms is still isolated to a few countries in a few sectors, but equity inflows and carry-trade activity are generally quite strong and these flows have to be watched carefully, particularly where leverage may be involved.

Policymakers will need to be attentive and act in a timely manner when pressures from inflows are building up, since policies take time to work. Those facing strong inflows and maintaining procyclical policies need to move to a neutral policy setting. Countries with undervalued exchange rates should allow this price mechanism to operate to help offset inflow pressures. However, if currency appreciation is not an option, other means such as monetary and/or fiscal policy should be deployed. Macroeconomic policy responses may, however, need to be complemented by strengthened macro-prudential measures (e.g., stricter loan to value ratios, funding composition restrictions) and, in some cases, capital controls.

Overall, while progress has been made and most financial sectors are on the mend, risks to global financial stability remain. Problems in Greece, and now Ireland, have reignited questions about sovereign debt sustainability and banking sector health in a broader set of euro-area countries and possibly beyond. The current detrimental interaction between financial system stability and sovereign debt sustainability needs to be dealt with in a comprehensive fashion, so as to break the adverse feedback loop that could spread beyond the smaller euro-area countries. Pressing forward with the regulatory reform agenda—for both institutions and markets— continues to be crucial. Without further progress in this field, global financial stability and sustainable growth will remain elusive.

Part 4   Reading Comprehension   阅读理解

Passage 1   International Financial Market 国际金融市场

Every country with a monetary system of its own has to have some kind of market in which dealers in bills, notes, and other forms of short term credit can buy and sell. The "money market" is a set of institutions or arrangements for handling what might be called wholesale transactions in money and short term credit. The need for such facilities arises in much the same way that a similar need does in connection with the distribution of any of the products of a diversified economy to their final users at the retail level. If the retailer is to provide reasonably adequate service to his customers, he must have active contacts with others who specialize in making or handling bulk quantities of whatever is his stock in trade. The money market is made up of specialized facilities of exactly this kind. It exists for the purpose of improving the ability of the retailers of financial services—commercial banks, savings institutions, investment houses, lending agencies, and even governments—to do their job. It has little if any contact with the individuals or firms who maintain accounts with these various retailers or purchase their securities or borrow from them.

The elemental functions of a money market must be performed in any kind of modern economy, even one that is largely planned or socialist, but the arrangements in socialist countries do not ordinarily take the form of a market. *Money markets exist in countries that use market processes rather than planned allocations to distribute most of their primary resources among alternative uses. The general distinguishing feature of a money market is that it relies upon open competition among those who are bulk suppliers of funds at any particular time and among those seeking bulk funds, to work out the best practicable distribution of the existing total volume of such funds.*

In their market transactions, those with bulk supplies of funds or demands for them, rely on groups of intermediaries who act as brokers or dealers. The characteristics of these middlemen, the services they perform, and their relationship to other parts of the financial vary widely from country to country. *In many countries there is no single meeting place where the middlemen get together, yet in most countries the contacts among all participants are sufficiently open and free to assure each supplier or user of funds that he will get or pay a price that fairly reflects all of the influences (including his own) that are currently affecting the whole supply and the whole demand.* In nearly all cases, moreover, the unifying force of competition is reflected at any given moment in a common price (that is, rate of interest) for similar transactions. Continuous fluctuations in the money market rates of interest result from changes in the pressure of available supplies of funds upon the market and in the pull of current demands upon the market.

1. The first paragraph is mainly about ( ).

   [A] the definition of money market

   [B] the constitution of a money market

   [C] the basic functions of a money market

   [D] the general feature of a money market

2. According to this passage, the money market ( ).

   [A] provides convenient services to its customers

   [B] has close contact with the individuals or firms seeking funds

   [C] maintains accounts with various retailers of financial services

   [D] is made up of institutions who specialize in handling wholesale monetary transactions

3. Which of the following statements concerning money market is not true according to this passage? ( )

   [A] Money market does not exist in planned economies

   [B] Money market has been established in some socialist countries

   [C] Money market encourages open competition among bulk suppliers of funds

   [D] Money market relies upon market processes to distribute funds to final users

4. The author uses the example of middleman to show (   ).

   [A] market transactions are important in different countries

   [B] dealers are needed in doing business

   [C] middlemen can play great role in different transactions and different countries

   [D] middlemen in different countries have different actions in business

5. According to this passage, (   ).

   [A] brokers usually perform the same kinds of services to their customers

   [B] brokers have little contact with each other

   [C] open competition tends to result in a common price for similar transactions at any given moment

   [D] changes in the pressure of available supplies of funds upon market tends to maintain a common price for similar transactions

Passage 2 A Strong Stock Market 强大的股票市场

The increase in the margin rate from 50% to 70% was not an attempt to stem any rampant speculation on the part of the public—actually the market seemed technically quite strong, with public participation essentially dignified—but rather an attempt by the Federal Reserve Board to preserve the sound underpinnings that existed in the market. Naturally, such a move had a momentarily chilling effect upon prices but if the FRB had been preoccupied with undue speculation, the increase might have been to the 80% or even 90% level. Such an increases in the margin rate is a confirmation of a strong stock market and since 1998, such increases have resulted in interim market highs over twelve months later. *Obviously, there could be no guarantee that this would once again be the case, but if history is any guideline—and if business and corporate earnings were to continue on the same course—continued optimism over the outlook for the stock market would seem more prudent than pessimism.*

The margin increase underscored the good rise that stocks had enjoyed for the previous year—and the fact that a 50% rate was maintained as long as it was pointed up the fact that the rise was mainly conservative in that it was concentrated in the blue chips for the most part. In past Investment Letters we have voiced the thought that speciality stocks could outperform the general market from this point. We continue to believe that this could be the case. For example, steel stocks tend to sell at certain fixed price/earnings ratios. Below a certain ratio they are considered good value—above a certain ratio, overpriced. If a company produces a unique product it is far more difficult for market analysis to place a numerical ratio upon the company's earnings. We have also contended in the past Letters that the stock market reflects mass psychology as well as the business outlook. When investors—both the public and the institutions—are nervous and pessimistic they definitely hesitate to buy stocks: they seek low price/earnings multiples and high yields. These same investors—when they are in an optimistic frame of mind—become for less preoccupied with yields and more willing to pay a premium(high p/e multiples) for accelerated growth. If the public's attitude towards the auto industry is any measure, then this period seems to have been one of optimism.

1. The title that best expresses the ideas of this passage is (　　).

    [A] A Time to Sell Stock

    [B] A Strong Stock Market

    [C] Raising the Margin Rate

    [D] Price/earnings Ratio in Steel

2. When investors are pessimistic what do they do? (　　)

    [A] They look to the FRB for help

    [B] They buy steel

    [C] They buy automobile stocks

    [D] They look for high yields

3. Why does the writer believe that speciality stocks could outperform the general market? (　　)

    [A] Because analysis have difficulty in deciding upon a fixed price/earnings ratio

    [B] Because the activity had been limited to blue chips

    [C] Because the rise was conservative

    [D] Because of the FRB action.

4. When investors are optimistic, what do they do? (　　)

    [A] They look for accelerated growth

    [B] They buy speciality stocks

    [C] They look for high yields

    [D] They are more prudent

Passage 3　The Falling U.S. Dollar 贬值的美元

Like a ticking time bomb, the falling dollar has grabbed the attention of Japan and West Germany, forcing them to consider adopting economic polices the United States advocates. The U.S. government wants the dollar to fall because as the dollar declines in value against the yen and Deutsche mark, U.S. good becomes cheaper. U.S. companies then sell more at home and abroad, and U.S. trade deficit declines. Cries for trade protection abate, and the global free-trade system is preserved.

Then, the cheaper dollar makes it cheaper for many foreign investors to snap up U.S. stocks.

That prompts heavy buying from abroad—especially from Japan. Also, if the trade picture is improving, that means U.S. companies eventually will be more competitive. Consequently, many investors are buying shares of export-oriented U.S. companies in anticipation of better profits in the next year or so. But that is a rather faddish notion right now; if corporate earnings are disappointing in interest rates, the stock market rally could stall.

Improving U.S. competitiveness means a decline in another's competitiveness.

Japan and West Germany are verging on recession. Their export-oriented economies are facing major problems. Japan is worried about the damage the strong yen will do to Japanese trade. West Germany is also worried. Share prices in Frankfurt plummeted this past week. Bonn is thought to be considering a cut in interest rates to boost its economy.

Could the falling dollar get out of hand? *If the dollar falls too far, investors might lose confidence in U.S. investments—especially the government bond market. The money to finance the federal budget and trade deficits could migrate elsewhere. Inflation could flare up, too, since Japanese and German manufacturers will eventually pass along price hikes—and U.S. companies might follow suit to increase their profit margins. The U.S. federal Reserve then might need to step in and stabilize the dollar by raising interest rates. And higher interest rates could cause the U.S. economy to slow down and end the Wall Street Rally.*

Worried about these side effects, Federal Reserve chairman Paul Volcher has said the dollar has fallen far enough. What is the equilibrium level? Probably near where it is or slightly lower. It all depends on when the U.S. trade deficit turns around or if investors defect from U.S. Treasury Bonds. "It requires a good deal of political patience on the part of the U.S. Congress", says Dr. Cline, "And there must be an expectation of patience on the part of private investors. The chance are relatively good that we will avoid an investor break or panic".

1. What is the main idea of this passage? (   )

    [A] The impression of the falling U.S. dollar

    [B] The result of the U.S. falling dollar

    [C] The side effect of U.S. falling dollar

    [D] Japan and West Germany are worried about U.S. falling dollar

2. What does the word "rally" mean? (   )

    [A] prosperity   [B] decline   [C] richness   [D] import

3. Why are Japan and West Germany worried about the falling dollar? (   )

    [A] Because the falling dollar may cause inflation in their countries

    [B] Because it may force them to sell a lot of U.S, stocks

    [C] Because it may do damage to their trade

    [D] Because it may make Japanese company less competitive

4. If dollar-falling got out of hand, and the U.S. Federal Reserve might step in , what would happen? (   )

    [A] The prosperity of the U.S. economy would disappear

    [B] The U.S. economy might face serious problems

    [C] Investors might lose confidence in U.S. investments

    [D]Inflation could flare up

Part 5　课 文 注 释

1. The goals of the IMF are to: ①promote international cooperation by providing the means for members to consult on international monetary issues; ②facilitate the growth of international payments; ③promote stability of exchange tares and seek the elimination of exchange restrictions that disrupt international trade; ④make short-term financial resources available to member countries on a temporary basis so as to allow them to correct payment disequilibrium without resorting to measures that would destroy national prosperity.

翻译：国际货币基金组织的目标是：①向成员国提供某种就国际货币问题相互协商的途径，以加强国际合作；②促进国际收支的增加；③稳定汇率，寻求消除阻碍国际贸易的外汇管制；④向成员国提供短期信贷，从而帮助这些国家改变其国际收支不平衡的状况，而不必采取损害其国民经济发展的措施。

2. The IMF can be thought of as a large group of nations that come together and combine resources. Over a given time period, some nations will face balance-of-payment surpluses while others will face deficits. The IMF can provide assistance by making available international reserves from the surplus nations to countries with temporary payment deficits.

翻译：可以说，国际货币基金组织是一个由多国组成的，把资金联合在一起的大型集团。在某一时期内，部分国家可能面临国际收支顺差，而另一部分国家则出现逆差。国际货币基金组织的作用在于获取顺差国家的国际储备,向国际收支暂时逆差的国家提供帮助。

3. All IMF loans are subject to some degree of conditionality. This means that in order to obtain a loan, a deficit nation must agree to implement economic and financial policies as stipulated by the IMF.

翻译：国际货币基金组织的所有贷款都是以遵循某些条款为条件的。也就是说，为了得到贷款，国际收支赤字的国家必须同意履行国际货币基金组织制定的经济和金融政策。

4. The IMF generally finances only a part of a member's payment deficits. In addition, IMF assistance is sometimes made in loose connection with World Bank lending, a portion of which can be used for balance-of-payments adjustment loans.

翻译：通常国际货币基金组织只是部分地资助某成员国的国际收支赤字。此外，国际货币基金组织的援助有时也同世界银行的贷款有所挂钩，即世界银行贷款的一部分也可以用于国际收支贷款的调节。

5. It is quite natural for a country to have disequilibrium in its international payment. If the country's export exceeds its import, that country enjoys a surplus in the international payments balance, which increases its gold and/ or foreign exchange reserves.

翻译：一个国家的国际收支出现不平衡是很自然的。如果出口大于进口，那么这个国家就享有国际收支的顺差，从而将会使其黄金或者外汇储备增加。

6. The size and terms and conditions of these foreign borrowings depend on the size and scale of the country's own gold and foreign exchange reserves. There are many different forms of these reserves, which are generally called international reserve.

翻译：一国能向国外借款规模的大小与借款条件的优劣，取决于本国黄金、外汇储备规模。所以在当今世界中，每个国家都必须保持一定数量的黄金、外汇储备。

7. The main functions of the international reserve: ①intervening the international exchange market to maintain the exchange rate of its currency; ②balancing short-term disequilibrium of its international payment; ③marketing it an important stand-by means of payments in its international trade; and ④increasing revenue by purchasing foreign state bonds and certificate of deposits.

翻译：国际储备的主要作用有：①干预外汇市场，保持其货币汇率；②平衡其国际收支出现的短期不平衡；③作为国际贸易中重要的备用国际支付手段；④以购买外国国库券和大额存单来增加收益。

8. Futures markets are centralized, regulated markets where an actual commodity is not physically traded; instead, futures contracts are bought and sold. Futures contracts are legally binding agreements and are standardized according to the quality, quantity, delivery time, and location for each commodity.

翻译：期货市场是集中化的、规范化的市场。在此市场中，交易的对象不是实际货物，而是买卖期货合约。期货合约是受到法律约束的、在质量、数量、交货时间及每一具体商品的交割地点上都有标准化的协议。

9. Options on futures, also traded on the floor of a regulated futures exchange, are contracts that convey the right, but not the obligation, to buy or sell a particular futures contract at a certain price for a limited time. Only the seller of the option is obligated to perform.

翻译：期权合约也在规范化的交易所内进行交易，它赋予买方权利，而不必负有义务，在某一限定时间内按某一特定价格水平买进或卖出某一相关期货合约，而期权卖方则必须根据买方要求履行合约。

10. Hedging is a two-step process. Depending upon a hedger's cash market situation, the hedger would either buy or sell futures as the first position. Then, at a later date, before the futures hedger would take a second position opposite the opening transaction.

翻译：套期保值交易运作分为两个阶段。套期保值者根据自己在现货市场的处境，可通过买进或卖出期货合约来建立第一个期货市场头寸。然后，在期货合约到期前的某一日，保值者将其原先持有的多头或者空头期货头寸通过做一次相反的交易而对冲。

11. Whether establishing a short or a long hedge, the main objective of hedging is to offset the price risk associated with buying, selling, or holding grain.

翻译：不论是建立空头套期保值，还是建立多头套期保值，套期保值交易的主要目的均为对冲伴随买入、卖出或持有商品期间因市场出现不利变动而引发的价格风险。

12. A share of stock represents ownership in a corporation. A corporation is owned by its stockholders—often thousands of people and institutions—each owing a fraction of the corporation.

翻译：股票的每一股代表着一家公司的一份股权。一家公司是由他的股票持有人——通常是成千上万的人和机构——（每一人或者每一机构拥有公司的一小部分）所拥有。

13. As a shareholder, you stand to profit when the company profit. You are also legally entitled to say in major policy decisions, such as whether to issue additional stock, sell the company to outside buyers, or change the board of directors. The rule is that each share has the same voting power, so the more share you own, the greater your power.

翻译：作为持股人，当公司盈利时你也可能获利，你可依法拥有在重大政策决策上的发言权，诸如是否追加发行股票，将公司出售给外部的买家，或变更董事会。按规定每一股拥有相同的表决权。因此，你拥有的股份越多，你的权利就越大。

14. The Balance of Payments (BOP) is a statistical statement that summarizes, for a specific period (typically a year or quarter), the economic transactions of an economy with the rest of the world.

翻译：国际收支是一定时期内(通常为一年或一个季度)一个国家(经济体)与世界其他经济体之间的经济交易的统计记录。

15. It is owned by the governments of 151 countries in the world, and its capital is subscribed by those governments. It provides funds to borrowers by borrowing funds in the world capital markets and from the proceeds of loan repayments as well as retained earnings.

翻译：世界银行由全世界 151 个会员国组成，其资金由会员国认购股份产生。世界银行从国际金融市场筹款，并用偿还的贷款以及其他收入向借贷者提供资金。

16. Given that the Bank's primary mission is to support the quality of life of people in developing member countries, it is easy to see why environmental and women's issues are receiving increasing attention.

翻译：众所周知，世界银行的最初任务是支持发展中成员国提高人民生活水平，这就不难看出环境和妇女项目为何得到越来越多的重视。

17. A stock does not have a fixed, objective worth. At any moment, it's only as valuable as people think it is.

翻译：股票没有一个固定的客观价值，在任意时刻，股票仅具有人们认为它所拥有的价值。

18. How do you judge a company's prospects? By current or anticipated earnings, the desirability of its product or service, competition, availability of new markets, management strengths and many other consideration. These are the factors that stock analysts track in trying to predict whether a stock's value will rise or fall.

翻译：你如何判断一个公司的前景？通过其当前的或预期的收益，对它的产品或服务的期望值，竞争性、新市场的可获得性、管理能力以及其他许多考虑因素。所有这些都是股票分析家们用于追踪并试图预测一只股票的价值将升或降的因素。

19. Every country with a monetary system of its own has to have some kind of market in which dealers in bills, notes, and other forms of short term credit can buy and sell. The "money market" is a set of institutions or arrangements for handling what might be called wholesale transactions in money and short term credit.

翻译：每一个拥有独立金融系统的国家都应该有这样的市场：在这里汇票、期票和其他形式的短期信贷可以进行买卖。"金融市场"就是一组用钱和短期信贷进行批发交易的公共机构或组织。

20. Money markets exist in countries that use market processes rather than planned allocations to distribute most of their primary resources among alternative uses. The general distinguishing feature of a money market is that it relies upon open competition among those who are bulk suppliers of funds at any particular time and among those seeking bulk funds, to work out the best practicable distribution of the existing total volume of such funds.

翻译：金融市场存在于那些利用市场而不是计划来分配资源的国家里。金融市场的基本特征是公平竞争，既存在于某一时间内资金的提供者之间，也存在于将这些资金合理分配的资金寻求者之间。

21. In many countries there is no single meeting place where the middlemen get together, yet in most countries the contacts among all participants are sufficiently open and free to assure each supplier or user of funds that he will get or pay a price that fairly reflects all of the influences (including his own) that are currently affecting the whole supply and the whole demand.

翻译：在许多国家，没有这些中间人聚集的专门地点，但大多数国家中所有参与者之间的联系都是公开进行，保证资金提供者和使用者在能正确了解目前影响供需的所有因素(包括他自身)的情况下买卖商品。

22. The increase in the margin rate from 50% to 70% was not an attempt to stem any rampant speculation on the part of the public—actually the market seemed technically quite strong, with public participation essentially dignified—but rather an attempt by the Federal Reserve Board to preserve the sound underpinnings that existed in the market.

翻译：保证金率从50%增长到70%，并不是想要遏制群众方面猖獗的投机，而是联邦储备委员会想要保持现存于股市强劲基础——事实上股市由于群众非常庄严的参与——在技术上看起来相当强劲。

23. Obviously, there could be no guarantee that this would once again be the case, but if history is any guideline—and if business and corporate earnings were to continue on the same course—continued optimism over the outlook for the stock market would seem more prudent than pessimism.

翻译：显然，不可能保证这种情况再次出现(情况再是这样)。可是，如果历史具有指导方针的话——如果商业和公司的利润仍然保持在同样轨道上——那么对股市前景乐观似乎要比悲观更精确些。

24. If the dollar falls too far, investors might lose confidence in U.S. investments—especially the government bond market. The money to finance the federal budget and trade deficits could migrate elsewhere. Inflation could flare up, too, since Japanese and German manufacturers will eventually pass along price hikes—and U.S. companies might follow suit to increase their profit margins. The U.S. Federal Reserve then might need to step in and stabilize the dollar by raising interest rates. And higher interest rates could cause the U.S. economy to slow down and end the Wall Street Rally.

翻译：如果美元下跌过多，投资者可能会失去对美国投资的信心，特别是对美国的债务市场。对联邦政府预算和贸易赤字提供的资金可能移向其他市场，因为日本和西德厂商最终会将上涨的价格转嫁出去，美国公司也可能这么做，以提高其市场利润幅度，从而使通货膨胀再次爆发。美国联邦储备委员会这时可能需要介入，提高利率来稳定美元。而较高利率会导致美国经济减慢，华尔街的繁荣行将结束。

25. Japan and West Germany are verging on recession. Their export-oriented economies are facing major problems. Japan is worried about the damage the strong yen will do to Japanese trade. West Germany is also worried. Share prices in Frankfurt plummeted this past week. Bonn is thought to be considering a cut in interest rates to boost its economy.

翻译：日本和西德正濒于经济衰退的边缘。其出口导向的经济正在面临严重问题。日本担心由于日元坚挺而给其贸易带来损害，西德也在发愁。上个星期，法兰克福股市价格暴跌。据说，波恩已在考虑降低利率以振兴其经济。

Part 6　词汇及扩展

International Monetary Fund 国际货币基金组织
balance of payment surplus 国际收支盈余
deficit 赤字
quota 份额、配额
floating rate 浮动利率
be subjected to 隶属于……，受……支配
International Reserve 国际储备
disequilibrium 失衡
foreign exchange capital 外汇资产
foreign exchange reserve 外汇储备
currency authority 货币当局
gold reserve 黄金储备
reserve position 储备头寸
stand-by means of payments 备用国际支付手段
state bonds 国库券
certificate of deposits 存单
General Drawing Rights 一般提款权
futures contract 期货合约
deliver time 交割时间
exchange trading floor 交易大厅
options on futures 期权
call option 看涨期权、买入期权
put option 看跌期权、卖出期权
hedging 套期保值
market option 市场头寸
hedger 套期保值者
opening position 多头
closing position 空头
a short hedge 空头套期保值
a long hedge 多头套期保值

shareholder 持股人
be entitled to 对……享有权利
the board of directors 董事会
absentee ballot 缺席者选票
proxy 代理人
Balance of Payment 国际收支
liabilities 负债
asset 资产
current account 经常账户
capital account 资本账户
financial account 金融账户
unilateral transfers 单方面转移
special drawing rights 特别提款权
foreign exchange 外汇
domestic interbank market 本国同业市场
broker 经纪人
International Bank for Reconstruction and Development 世界复兴开发银行
be subscribed by 由……认捐、赞助
retained earnings 未分配盈余
Marshall Plan 马歇尔计划
a grace period 宽限期
convertible currencies 可兑换通货
long-term rates 长期贷款利率
margin rate 保证金率，边际比率
rampant 无约束力，猖獗的，蔓延的
interim 间歇；暂时的，间歇的
guideline 方针，指导路线
blue-chip 蓝筹股票
overprice 将……标价过高
numerical ratio 数率，数字比率
earnings 收益，利润，收入
premium 佣金，酬金
snap up 争购，抢购
heavy buying 大量买进

export-oriented 出口导向的
buying spree 狂购乱买
stall 停滞
verging on recession 正处于衰退的边缘
boost 振兴，吹捧
bond market 债券市场
profit margin 利润幅度
break or panic 崩溃或大恐慌
cries for trade protection 贸易保护的呼声
the global free-trade system 全球自由贸易体系
trade deficit 贸易赤字，贸易逆差

Part 7 网络学习资源

1. 经济分析局搜集有关美国的国际收支、进出口、国际投资状况的资料，可以登录 www.bea.doc.gov 直接链接到相关事业信息的网站。

2. Wells Fargo 银行的网址提供其国际业务部的汇率和国际外汇交易信息。浏览该网页可登录 www.wellsfargo.com。

3. 彭博是一家著名的金融服务公司，其网址提供主要国家的货币汇率信息。网址为 www.bloomberg.com。

4. 在圣路易斯联邦储备银行的网页上可以查到一些有关汇率的历史资料。为得到汇率和国际收支的数据可登录 www.stls.frb.org。

5. 太平洋汇率服务公司提供当天的汇率信息，还有加元通其他 5 种主要货币间汇率的预期。网址为 http://pacific.commerce.ubc.ca/xr。

6. 国外关系委员会是一个专门研究和讨论美国在全球经济中的作用的政府机构。了解国际金融和贸易方面的近期研究，可以登录 www.cfr.org/p/。

Unit 4   International Cooperation and Transnational Corporation 国际合作与跨国公司

Part 1   Intensive Reading   精读

Passage 1   The Joint International Venture 国际合资企业

The term "joint international business venture", joint venture for short, has come to mean many things to many people. It sometimes is taken to mean any joint relationship between one or more foreign firms and one or more local firms. Such a broad definition is excluded here. *Joint ownership of an operation in which at least one of the partners is foreign based.*

Joint ventures can take many forms. A foreign firm may take a majority share, a minority share, or an equal share in ownership. While it is not necessary to have financial control or to have operating control, some firms refuse to use the joint venture form if it is not possible to have a majority position in ownership. There are firms that have few qualms about holding minority position, however, so long as they can have operating control. They achieve this through technical-aid, management, or supply contracts.

It should be recognized that maintaining operating control is sometimes difficult if one does not have financial control too. Objectives of the participants may diverge; when they do, financial control becomes important. *Management may wish to reinvest earnings while the majority of the board may wish earnings distributed as dividends.* Unless policy issues of this kind can be settled amicably, lack of financial control can prove to be very unsatisfactory, if not fatal.

Many joint ventures emerge as matters of necessity: that is, no single firm is willing to assume the risks entailed, while a consortium of firms is. Large, capital-intensive, long-lived investments are natural candidates for the joint-venture. Exploitation of resource deposits often is done by a consortium of several petroleum or mining firms. Roles are parceled out even though each phase of the operation is owned jointly. One firm does the actual mining, another provides transportation, and still another does the refining and extraction. There is a wide variety of combinations. An example, as shown in Table 4-1, indicates some of the possibilities. Each of three firms contributes roughly one-third of the total investment. None has operating control of the aggregate investment, but each has operating control of that part of the total in which its expertise is dominant. This assures that on decisions affecting the total operation each firm is treated equally. Decisions that affect one part of system are made by the firm most knowledgeable in that field.

Table 4-1 Ownership Pattern of a Large Joint Venture

Phase of Operation	Mining Firm (%)	Transportation Firm (%)	Refining Firm (%)	Value in Millions of $
Mining	51	19	30	1000
Transportation	20	60	20	500
Refining	15	30	55	300
Total	36.4	32.2	31.4	1800

The example illustrates the type of joint venture that firms consciously wish to undertake. *However, increasingly, joint ventures are an extension of nationalism and are undertaken as a condition of entry rather than as a permissive arrangement between firms.* Several countries now require that there be local ownership participation in new venture involving foreign equity capital. In some instance: national governments insist on local financial control in a few industrial sectors. In others, almost all new investments must have at least 50 percent local participation. Countries that currently require local equity participation in some industries and in some form include India, Peru, the Philippines, Malaysia, and Indonesia.

As noted, the joint venture can pose problems, especially if it is an enforced marriage of partners. For many ventures in small countries, it is difficult to find a suitable local partner, that is, one with sufficient capital and know-how to be able to contribute to the partnership. In some developing countries, a small handful of families control the entire locally-owned part of the industrial structure. Under these circumstances, a jont venture merely insulates them further from independent, foreign-owned plants that would compete against them. For this and other reasons, the only suitable partner may end up being the government itself. Most multinational firms, however, shy away from such arrangements where possible.

The Japanese multinational firms are much more likely to engage in joint venture than are European and American firms. One explanation for this is that the Japanese are the new comers on the international scene. And have had to enter most countries under more stringent conditions than did the European and American firms. Also, the large bulk of Japanese investments (55 percent of the total and 72 percent of manufacturing investments) are located in developing countries where joint ventures are preferable to wholly-owned subsidiaries. U.S.-based firms, by contrast, have only

21 percent of their investments in developing countries and 79 percent in advanced countries. Also, over 60 percent of U.S.-owned investments in manufacturing in developing countries are concentrated in high-technology fields, whereas Japanese firms have about two-third of them manufacturing investment in developing countries located in relatively low-technology industries. Since Japanese firms may have less to protect in the way of technology, they compete in the same willing to share ownership. Also, they compete in the same industries as do local firms and hence may feel compelled to use joint ventures as a form of protective coloration.

Passage 2 International Technological Transfer 国际技术转让

International transfers of technology have increased substantially in the postwar period. The major flow of technology has been among firms in the industrialized countries, but technological transfer between firms in the industrialized, market-oriented economies and firms in the developing countries and the centrally planned countries has been growing in the last two decades, and should continue to grow during the 1980s. This growth has several reasons. The developing countries have become increasingly aware of the role of technology in fostering economic development and the ability to complete in international production. The centrally planned economies will continue their effort to attain technological self-sufficiency during the 1980s, and in the process, the flow of technology to them from the industrial market economies should accelerate.

The transnational enterprises (TNEs) play a central role in the transfer of technology and the rate of technological diffusion. The greater part of the technology transferred among firms in the industrial market economies involves advanced systems of the TNEs. *The dominant channel of transfer is through world trade. Direct forms of transfer include licenses, patents, sale of technological know-how, and direct investment. Firms in the industrialized countries increasingly use a combination of these channels to gain new technological expertise.*

Meanwhile, the politics of economic cooperation between the Western market economics and the Eastern, centralized economies that has prevailed for the past two decades has provided opportunities for trade between these two groups, and along with the trade has come the transfer of technology. In addition, the rapid expansion of trade between the industrialized economics and the developing countries, and the increased flow of foreign direct investment to the developing countries, have also provided channels for the transfer of technology needed by these counties for industrialization and development.

International Cooperation and Transnational Corporation 国际合作与跨国公司

1. Principal Methods of Transferring Technology

As noted previously, the three principal methods available to the transnational enterprises(TNEs) for the transfer of technology abroad are exporting, direct investment, and licensing arrangements.

Most technological transfer among firms in different countries takes place through the exporting and importing activities of world trade. The rate of technological diffusion, therefore, has increased with the rapid growth of world trade in the last two decades. *Technological transfers through trade range from simple products to the highly sophisticated technological systems normally traded between firms in the industrialized countries.* Transactions involving the sale of advanced technological systems usually contain arrangements for cooperation in production and for transfer of technological know-how and patent rights to the foreign firm buying the system.

Direct investment in foreign subsidiaries is a channel frequently used by U.S. firms to transfer technology abroad. A U.S. parent company will provide its foreign subsidiaries with the technology needed for use in its manufacturing operations. The parent company will usually also have to provide technical and general management skills as well as marketing expertise and training facilities for the local work force.

U.S. firms generally use licensing arrangements to transfer technology to unaffiliated foreign firms. In the protected Japanese market, for example, restrictions on direct investments and protective tariff barriers on imports make licensing arrangements the most effective means of entry of U.S. companies.

2. Rates of Diffusion

The rate of diffusion varies with the type of technology and is determined by the degree of difficulty of transfer. The costs of transferring the technology increase with the difficulty. The three board types of technology are ①general technology, ②firm-specific technology, and ③system-specific technology. *General technology involves information that is common to an industry or trade and represents the general state of technological knowledge in the industry or trade.* The technology that forms the basis of a whole industry is complex, which makes general technology the most difficult type to transfer to another country.

Firm-specific technology refers to technology specific to a particular firm's experience, activities, and know-how, but not attributable to any specific item the firm products. The diffusion rate of firm-specific technology is higher than that of general technology.

System-Specific technology concerns the technology used in the production of a production of a product by all manufacturers within the industry. This is the least difficult of the three types of technology to transfer, and thus it has the highest rate of technological diffusion.

Passage 3 Transnational Corporations 跨国公司

The significance of transnational corporation, specially the large global corporation, lies mainly in three basic characteristics.

① Its control of economic activities in more than one country.

② Its ability to take advantage of geographical differences between countries and regions in factor endowments (including government polices).

③ Its geographical flexibility, that is, its ability to shift its resources and locations at a global scale.

Hence, much of the changing shape of the global economic system is sculptured by the TNC through its decisions to invest or not to invest in particular geographical locations. It is moulded, too, by the resulting flows of materials, component and finished products as well as of technological and organizational expertise between geographically dispersed operations. Although the relative importance of TNCs varies considerably—from industry to industry, from country to country and between different parts of the world in which TNC influence, whether direct or indirect, is not important. In some cases, indeed, the influence of TNCs on an area's economic fortunes can be overwhelming.

One way of defining a transnational is in terms of its ownership of overseas assets and activities, where such ownership confers control over the overseas operation. This is the definition used in all national statistical sources, although the precise percentage of ownership used varies from country to country (this creates one of the many problems involved in making international comparisons of TNC activity).

As will become clear in subsequent chapters, there are many ways—direct or indirect, financial and non-financial—in which a business may be regarded as transnational in its activities, behavior and influence on national and local economies. A more satisfactory and more comprehensive definition of a transnational corporation is that suggested by Cowling and Sugden: *A transnational is the means of co-coordinating production from one center of strategic decision making when this co-coordinating takes a firm across national boundaries.* A broader definition of this kind is necessary to capture the increasing diversity in the forms of international involvement used by business firms. Many of these forms do not involve ownership or equity relationships but are, rather, various forms of collaboration between legally corporation independent firms in different countries. Unfortunately, there are no comprehensive, internationally comparable statistical data to match the broader definition of a transnational corporation. In trying to obtain an idea of the general growth and spread of TNCs we have to use the foreign direct investment data collected (very unevenly) by national governments.

Unit 4
International Cooperation and Transnational Corporation 国际合作与跨国公司

TNCs are responsible for a disproportionate share of world employment, production and trade. Between one-fifth and one-quarter of total world production in the world's market economics is performed by TNCs. Such a large share of world production, together with the geographical extensiveness of their operation—their "global reach" also makes them an increasingly dominant force in world trade. In other words, it is trade that takes place between parts of the same firm but across national boundaries. Unlike the kind of trade assumed in international trade theory, intra-firm trade does not take place on an: "arm's length" basis. *It is, therefore, not subject to external market prices but to the internal decisions of TNCs.*

In effect, international trade in manufactured goods looks less and less like the trade of basic economic models in which buyers and sellers interact freely with one another (*in reasonably competitive markets*) *to establish the volume and prices of traded goods.* It is increasingly managed by multinational corporations as part their systems of international production and distribution.

Such trade may account for a very large share of a nation's exports and imports. In fact, very few countries collect trade statistics in such a way that intra-firm trade can be distinguished from total trade flows. However such evidence, as does exist is at least suggestive of the very important proportion of world trade which is carried on within the boundaries of TNCs. For example, more than 50 percent of the total trade which is carried on within the boundaries of TNCs. Possibly as much as four-fifths of the United Kingdom's manufactured exports are flows of intra-firm trade either within UK enterprises with foreign affiliates or within foreign-controlled enterprises with operations in the United Kingdom.

The conventional image of the TNCs tends to be narrow and stereotyped. Mention of the term "transnational" or "multinational" enterprise immediately evokes the picture of a gargantuan organization—an IBM or an ICI, a Unilever or Philips, a General Electric or a Ford—whose activities encircle the globe and penetrate its remotest reaches. Such TNCs are, indeed, the dominant forces in the world economy. They are, as is so often pointed out, broadly equivalent in economic terms to some entire nations. As Benson and Lloyd point out, of the 100 largest economic units in the world today, half are nation-states and the other half TNCs. In fact, only perhaps 4 or 5 percent of the total population of TNCs the world can be regarded as truly global corporations. But, their sheer individual magnitude gives them a significance out of all proportion to their numbers. For example, some three-quarters of the United State's transnational activity is performed by fewer than 300 firms; four-fifths of UK direct investment abroad is in the hands of around 150 firms.

The United Nations Center on Transnational Corporations (UNCTC) has identified a core of

600 transnational corporations in mining and manufacturing with annual sales of more than $1 billion in 1985. This "billion dollar club" created more than one-fifth of the total industrial and agricultural production in the world's market economies. Of the 600, a mere 74 TNCs accounted for 50 percent of the total sale. In addition to these 600 TNCs, the UNCTC also identified a further 365 major TNCs in business services. In an investigation on some leading manufacturing TNCs in 1989, statistic results indicates the varied extent of transnationality even among the largest firms. For example, motor vehicle manufacturers figure prominently as major TNCs but they are not all equally involved in foreign production. Similar variation is apparent in other sectors such as chemicals and electrical production. *Even so, the degree of foreign involvement by these giant firms is extremely high. In addition, during the postwar period the leading TNCs have become increasingly global in their production.*

Part 2　Extensive Reading　泛读

Passage 1　Economic Policy of Open Economy 开放的经济政策

1. Economic Goals of Nations

In an open economy, we can summarize the desirable economic goals as being the attainment of internal balance and external balance. Internal balance means a steady growth of the domestic economy consistent with a low unemployment rate. It implies full employment and stable prices. External balance is the achievement of a desired trade balance or desired international capital flows. A nation is said to be in external balance when the current account is neither so deeply in deficit that the home nation is not incapable of repaying its foreign debts in the future nor so strongly in surplus that foreign nations can not repay their debts to it.

In practice, these two definitions are both unable to include all potential policy goals, such as long-run economic growth, a reasonable equitable distribution of national income. However, the definitions of internal balanced and external balanced have summarized the common goals of most policy makers. The discussion in this chapter is confined to the pursuit of internal balance and external balance.

2. Policy Instruments

To attain the objectives of external balance and internal balance, policy makers adopt the following policy instruments.

(1) Expenditure-changing Policies

Expenditure-changing policies include fiscal policy, which refers to changes in government taxes and spending; and monetary policy, which refers to changes in the money supply by a nation's central bank.

(2) Expenditure-switching Policies

Expenditure-switching policies refer to changes in the exchange rate (i.e., a devaluation or revaluation). Under a system of fixed exchange rates, a trade-deficit nation could devalue its currency to increase the international competitiveness of its industries, thus diverting spending from foreign goods to domestic goods. To increase its competitiveness under a managed floating exchange-rate system, the nation could purchase other currencies with its domestic currency, thereby causing the exchange value of its currency to depreciate. Thus, a deficit in the nation's balance of payments is corrected and domestic production is increased. The success of these policies in promoting trade balance largely depends on switching demand in the proper direction and amount, as well as on the capacity of the home economy to meet the additional demand by supplying more goods.

(3) Direct Controls Consist

Direct controls consist of government restrictions on the market economy. They are tariffs, quotas, and other restrictions on the flow of international trade and capital. They are selective expenditure-switching policies whose objective is to control particular items in the balance of payments.

3. Policy Effects

(1) Monetary Policy and Fiscal Policy: Effects on Internal Balance

Let us now consider fiscal policy and monetary policy which are generally used to have effects on both internal sector and external sector. Assume that international capital mobility is perfect. This suggests that a small change in the relative interest rate across nations induces a large international flow of capital (investment funds). This assumption is consistent with capital movements among many industrial nations.

① Monetary policy under fixed exchange rates.

We assumed that a nation was experiencing domestic recession and that it allowed its currency to fix in the foreign exchange market. To stimulate domestic economy, the central bank adopts an expansionary monetary policy. The monetary expansion reduces interest rates, leading to rising aggregate demand, output, and employment. Lower interest rates result in large capital outflows and depreciation of the domestic currency on foreign exchange market. To maintain a fixed exchange rate, however, the central bank intervenes and sells foreign currency to buy domestic currency. This decreases the domestic money supply and offsets the initial increase in the money supply. The initial output and employment expansion resulting from the expansionary monetary policy is blunted, and internal balance is not attained. Thus, monetary policy under fixed exchange rates is ineffective in promoting internal balance.

② Fiscal policy under fixed exchange rates.

Suppose that a nation operates under a fixed exchange-rate system and encounters domestic recession. Let us follow the case of an expansionary fiscal policy, such as a tax cut or increased government spending. The rise in government spending increases aggregate demand and result in a higher domestic income level. As total spending rises, so does the demand for money. Given the supply of money, interest rates increase. This encourages foreigners to invest more in the home nation and discourages its residents from investing abroad. The resulting net capital inflows push the nation's capital account into surplus. Concurrently, the increase in spending results in higher imports and a trade deficit. If investment flows are highly mobile, it is likely that the capital account surplus will exceed the trade-account deficit; the overall BOP thus moves into surplus. To stop the domestic currency from appreciating, the central bank must increases the money supply and buys foreign currency with domestic money. This leads to additional spending, output, and employment. In this manner, the expansionary fiscal policy promotes internal balance. With fixed exchange rates and perfect capital mobility, fiscal policy will have a strong effect on income and can be used to stimulate the domestic economy.

③ Monetary policy under floating exchange rates.

Suppose that a nation adopts an expansionary monetary policy with floating exchange rates. With a floating exchange-rates system, the central bank is not obliged to intervene in the foreign-exchange market to support a particular exchange rate. With no intervention, the current account surplus (deficit) will always equal the capital account deficit (surplus) so that the official settlements balance equals zero. In addition, since the central bank does not intervene to fix the exchange rate, the money supply can change to any level desired by the monetary authorities. This independence of monetary policy is one of the advantages of floating exchange rates. By increasing the money supply relative to the money demand, the monetary policy leads to lower interest rates, which stimulate aggregate demand and output. Lower interest rates also discourage foreigners from investing in the home currency and encourage its residents to invest abroad, causing a larger capital account deficit (official settlements deficit). Since this is a floating exchange rate system, the official settlements deficit is avoided by the adjustment exchange rate to a level that restores equilibrium. The pressure of the official settlements deficit will cause the domestic currency to depreciate. This depreciation is associated with domestic net exports increase which leads to further increases in output and employment. The expansionary monetary policy thus promotes internal balance. In contrast to the fixed exchange rates world, money policies can change the level of income with floating exchange rates.

④ Fiscal policy under floating exchange rates.

We now consider the effects of an expansionary fiscal policy under floating exchange rates. Fiscal expansion leads to higher output and income as well as higher interest rates. Higher income induces rising imports, which push the trade account into deficit. Higher interest rates lead to net investment inflows and a surplus in the capital account. With highly mobile capital, it is likely that the surplus in the capital account will exceed the deficit in the trade account, so that the overall BOP moves into surplus. Since the exchange rate is free to adjust to eliminate the BOP surplus, the exchange rate will appreciate. With a floating exchange—rate system, the central bank does nothing to offset this appreciation. This appreciation will reduce domestic exports and increase imports. With floating exchange rates, fiscal policy has no effect on income. Complete crowding out has occurred. This crowding out occurs because the currency appreciation induced by the expansionary fiscal policy reduces net exports to a level that just offsets the positive fiscal policy effects on income.

(2) Monetary Policy and Fiscal Policy: Effects on External Balance

We assume that the exchange rate is fixed, because BOP surpluses and BOP deficits are issues only when the exchange rate is fixed; recall that floating exchange rates automatically adjust to promote BOP equilibrium.

The short-run effects of monetary policy on the BOP are definite: An expansion in the money supply worsens the BOP, whereas a contraction in the money supply improves the BOP.

To illustrate, suppose the central bank increases the money supply, relative to the money demand, which pushes interest rates downward. Falling interest rates encourage additional investment spending, which results in an increase in domestic income level. The rise in income, in turn, increases imports and worsens the trade balance. At the same time, falling interest rates (relative to those abroad) induce net investment outflows and deterioration in the capital account. By worsening the trade-account balance and capital account balance, the monetary expansion worsens overall BOP. In the long run, the overseas investments will be repaid with interest, resulting in a positive feedback into the BOP; but the negative effect on the trade balance will persist.

The short-run effects on the BOP of expansionary fiscal policy are not as clear as those of monetary policy. Assume the government increases its purchases of goods and services, leading to increases in aggregate demand, output, and income. Rising income, in turn, induces rising imports and a worsening trade balance. Meanwhile, increased government spending increases money demand and raises interest rates. The higher interest rates, in turn, induce net investment inflows and an improvement in the capital account. If capital mobility is sufficiently high, the improvement in the capital account more than offsets the trade account deterioration, and the overall BOP improves. Eventually, however, foreign investors must be repaid with interest, and this more than offsets the investment inflows caused by higher interest rates. As a result, the fiscal expansion probably worsens the overall BOP in the long run, albeit improving it in the short run if enough investment inflows occur in response to higher interest rates.

4. International Policy Coordination

International economic policy coordination is the attempt to significantly modify national policies (monetary policy, fiscal policy, exchange-rate policy) in recognition of international economic interdependence. Against the background of economic globalization, economic policies of one nation have spillover effects on others. To make economic policies effective, a great deal of international cooperation is required. The basic argument in favor of international policy coordination is that such coordination would stabilize exchange rates. Whether or not exchange rate stability offers any substantial benefits over freely floating rates with independent policies is a matter of much debate. Some experts argue that coordinated monetary policy to achieve fixed exchange rates or to reduce exchange rate fluctuations to within narrow "target zones" would reduce the destabilizing aspects of international trade in goods and financial assets when currencies become "overvalued"or "undervalued". This view emphasizes that in an increasingly integrated world economy, it seems desirable to conduct national economic policy in an international context rather than to simply focus on domestic policy goals without considering the international implications.

Aside from exchange rate objectives, international policy coordination may involve other macroeconomic objectives that take into consideration the interdependent nature of the global economy. One example is the avoidance of so-called beggar-thy-neighbor policies whereby a country will devalue its currency to stimulate its exports and discourage imports. If other countries respond by devaluing their currencies, then the series of competitive devaluations will end with the devaluations. Such competitive devaluations may be avoided through the international coordination of policies where it is made clear that individual countries will not find beggar-thy-neighbor policies successful. In the Plaza Accord of 1985, Germany and Japan agreed to adopt stimulative fiscal policy to promote imports from the U.S. and to intervene in foreign currency markets to further depreciation in the U.S. and to intervene in foreign currency markets to further depreciation in the dollar's exchange value. To facilitate policy coordination, economic officials of the major governments talk with each other frequently in the context of IMF and the OECD. There are many examples of international economic policy coordination.

Although the benefits from international economic coordination are obvious, several obstacles have hindered successful policy coordination. Many leading economists have participated, but a problem at the practical level is that different governments emphasize different goals and may view the current economic situation differently.

Passage 2 Open China Economy 开放的中国经济

China's opening to the outside world has been an integral part of the process of economic reform and transformation underway since 1978. Two areas related to China's economic growth deserve special recognition and analysis: international trade and foreign investment. They are the two most important forces related to external factors behind China's economic reform and have contributed significantly to China's economic growth, which are driven by both internal and external factors. On December 11, 2001, China became a member of the WTO, China's entry into the WTO will make China's door even more open. Both foreign investment and foreign trade are expected to increase.

1. International Trade

(1) Rapid Growth and Structural Change in Chinese Foreign Trade

Before the process of economic opening began during the 1970s, China was one of the most closed economies in the world. In 1971, the low point of China's integration into the global economy, total exports and imports accounted just under 5% of China's GDP, it has surged more than 40% of China's GDP today. Foreign trade has been an important component of Chinese economy.

In 1978, at the beginning of the economic reform, China's exports to the world were US$ 9.8 billion. It was ranked 32nd in the world total exports of US$ 1,242 billion. However, In 2004, China's exports and imports were 1,154.7 billion, exports rose 35.4% to 593.3 billion, imports rose 36% to US$561.4 billion, trade surplus rose 25.4% to US$31.9 billion, China's exports represented about 6.5% of the world total exports, China was now ranked number third in the world. Between 1981 and 2004, exports grew at 15.26% annually (nominal value), while imports grew at 15.12% per year. This remarkable accomplishment and improved ranking have demonstrated successes of China's economic reform and the rising power of China's trade position in the global.

Along with quantitative growth has come dramatic structural change. The most important change in exports has been a dramatic shift to labor intensive commodities, and a correspondingly large decline in natural resource-based products. In 1985, primary products accounted for 51% of Chinese export commodities. However, in 2003, 92% of China's exports commodities were labor-intensive manufactured goods. By 2004, the mechanical and electrical product exports were US$ 323.4 billion, accounted for 54.5% of the total exports, among them, the high-tech product exports were US$ 165.54 billion, and accounted for 27.9% of the total exports, the transition out of labor intensive products has already begun.

While the composition of China's exports has shifted to much better reflect China's abundant labor endowment, imports have continued to be concentrated in capital and technology-intensive products. Capital intensive products accounted for 58.6% of total imports in 2004. In addition, resource products imports increased obviously, fertilizer, crude oil, food grains, synthetic fiber materials, and iron ore, each of which imports increased 30% in 2004. Chinese trade structure overwhelmingly corresponds to comparative advantage principles.

(2) The Process of Trade Reform

The Chinese foreign-trade system in the late 1970s closely followed the model of other centrally-planned economies. The domestic economy was rigorously separated from the world economy through a centrally-controlled foreign trade monopoly. Direct control over the physical commodities entering into trade was exercised by a few national foreign trade companies. In addition, the Chinese currency was not convertible: private individuals had no right to exchange domestic for foreign currencies, and the currency value was set by government officials. The system was rigid because there were overlapping, redundant controls covering both the flow of goods and the flow of money.

Beginning in 1978, the government gradually dismantled this system of overlapping administrative controls and set up a system in which most trade is governed by market forces. The main elements included the following.

① Devaluation.

By 1987, the real exchange rate was down to about 40 (1980=100), a level it roughly maintained in subsequent years. This set the scene for the restructuring of output and trade in subsequent years.

② Movement towards currency convertibility.

During 1996, current account convertibility was achieved. Any authorized importer of goods and services can purchase foreign exchange upon presentation of documentation of the trade flows. However, access to foreign exchange to transfer funds across borders for private purposes is not generally available. The government trades foreign exchange through the (state-run) banking system.

International Cooperation and Transnational Corporation 国际合作与跨国公司 Unit 4

③ Demonopolization of the foreign trade regime.

Local affiliates were permitted to set up as independent corporations, and local governments and SEZs were allowed to set up trading companies. Equally importantly, changes in the domestic economy began to give firms (both production enterprises and trading companies) much stronger incentives to find profitable business.

④ Reduction in Non-tariff Barriers (NTBs).

In the old system, all trade was covered by NTBs. From the late 1980s, NTBs began to be substantially reduced, although not entirely eliminated.

⑤ Pricing principles were significantly changed.

As domestic reforms changed the basis for pricing to a market system, so the foreign trade system steadily adopted systems that transmitted world price signals through to the domestic economy.

(3) Creation of Export Promotion (EP) Regime

Since 1978, China has established the EP regime, Chinese export success has been dependent on it. There were two crucial elements to the establishment of the EP regime in China. The first was the permission, legal framework, and concessionary taxation policies granted to encourage foreign investors to establish export-oriented firms in China. The second was the establishment of a program of export-processing, under which inputs and components for export production were imported duty-free, with a minimum of administrative interference. The EP regime has been part of a program of trade reform that has reshaped every aspect of China's foreign trade. The striking outcome of EP regime is that FIEs can come into Chinese domestic market literally, and then be the motor of China's export expansion. Foreign investment has played the key role in China's exports since 1992. In 2004, The FIEs' exports accounted for 54.8% of China's exports, their imports accounted for 56.2% of China's imports. With the flood of foreign investment into China after 1992, China's export has grown rapidly. Since labor-intensive manufactured exports mostly came from FIEs, the trade structure has been improved. China's export growth and upgrading resulting from EP regime are likely of enormous benefits to the Chinese domestic economy.

(4) Future Prospects for China's Trade

China's rapid growth will continue, future growth of trade will follow WTO membership. In part, this is because broad liberalization will reduce China's costs and improve competitiveness. In addition, some of the quantitative restraints that hold back China's exports will be phased out. Further stages of integration with the world economy will occur, bringing substantial benefits to China. Its labor-rich, land-scarce, and capital-scarce economy can benefit from comparative advantage.

2. Foreign Investment

As late as 1970s, China was closed to foreign investment. In 1978, the decision was made to accept foreign investment; SEZs were established in 1979 and 1980. Incoming FDI grew steadily through the 1980s, from 1993 onward, the stream of incoming FDI turned into a flood. The amount of FDI flows into Mainland China has increased almost 40 times from 1984 to 2003. From 1993 onward, China became the largest recipient of incoming FDI among developing countries, and second to U.S. in the world. During the 1990s and continuing into the current decade, foreign investment had a profound and fundamental impact on the Chinese economy. They contributed to the following areas such as: ①half of China's exports; ②facilitating advanced technology transfer to China; ③forming a manufacturing base to utilize China's cheap labor, etc. Although FDI has brought benefits to China, there are some potential costs to China: Foreign firms have gained more control of products through their market power over time or could use their comparative advantages to drive out local competitors, leading to a potential shrinking of indigenous industries; Foreign firms may use transfer-pricing strategies to avoid paying taxes to China.

(1) Liberalization of the Investment Regime

Under the "open door" policy introduced in 1978, the Chinese government adopted new policies, and authorized policy experimentation in the two southern provinces of Guangdong and Fujian, giving them a high degree of flexibility with regard to budgetary, foreign trade, and foreign investment policy. Four SEZs were established in 1979 and 1980, they were regions in which foreign investment was encouraged by lower tax rates, few administrative restrictions, and simplified customs procedures. The second wave of liberalization began in 1984; fourteen new "open cities" were designated, ranging from Dalian in the north, to Beihai in the south. The 14 cities were all authorized to set up special zones that offered foreign investors some of the same preferential treatment available in the SEZs. After 1985, a series of measures were taken to rehabilitate the foreign investment regime. First, FIEs were given access to a secondary market for foreign exchange. Second, future liberalization of the legal regime governing FIEs took place. Third, "Coastal Development Strategy" was adopted. Shandong and Liaodong peninsulas were declared open areas, entire coastal region were opened to the outside world. These open areas were granted preferential policies—lower taxes for foreign and domestic investors, export/import powers, and freedom to raise capital which cut transaction costs and improved their comparative advantage. These policies were important and successful. The third wave of liberalization began

Unit 4

International Cooperation and Transnational Corporation 国际合作与跨国公司

in 1992—1993, China undertook a number of measures: created a new "special zone" in Shanghai, at Pudong; the interior cities were opened to the outside world; new sectors, especially real estate were opened to foreign investment; Manufacturers were granted rights to sell their output on the Chinese market, etc. These measures sent a strong message that investment was welcomed, and that administrative restrictions were being reduced. After 1993, incoming FDI increased rapidly.

(2) Source of FDI in China

The factor that fueled China's success in attracting FDI was the country's immense comparative advantage. Significant differences in the value of goods and services inside and outside China, created by decades of economic austerityand cheap labor, meant that those who could move goods, services, technology or themselves across China's borders could earn large profits in either the domestic or international market. Substantial inflows of investment from developed countries helped China improve technological capacities and move into production and export of commodities at much higher technological levels. It is an undeniable fact that foreign investment has made massive contributions to China.

Part 3 Academic Reading 学术阅读

**Passage Host Country Resource Availability and Resource Dependence Theory
母国资源的可获得性与资源依赖理论**

The management of the information systems (IS) function is a complex task, particularly in the case of multinational corporations (MNCs), where installations dispersed across distance, time, and cultures can lead to diverse and incompatible systems spreading among foreign subsidiaries. The need to globally control and coordinate the IS management function is often met with resistance from local IS managers, who may perceive corporate standards as intrusive. Resource dependence theory (RDT) argues that control is made easier when a subsidiary unit is dependent on corporate headquarters for critical resources. This study examined the IS management relationship and the use of various mechanisms of control (formal and informal) between 54 headquarters—subsidiary pairs spread across 19 countries of varying resource-richness. While RDT appears to be valid when subsidiaries are dependent on MNC headquarters for resources, the expected relationship between the mechanisms and host country IS resource availability was not observed. Although there was a significant relationship with the use of informal mechanisms and IS resources, it was in the opposite direction to what would be expected by RDT.

The scale is staggering. General Electric, a diversified technology and services company, currently has operations in over 100 countries and employs nearly 315,000 employees worldwide. On its corporate Web site, Swiss giant Nestlé S.A. boasts of having factories in nearly every country of the world. Toyota Motor Corporation, Japan's largest multinational, has manufacturing plants spread across 26 nations supporting the efforts of its 246,700 global employees. These companies are not alone in their astounding breadth of operations. The *World Investment Report 2005,* published by the United Nations Conference on Trade and Development (UNCTAD), estimates that there are currently over 70,000 multinational corporations (MNCs) operating worldwide, controlling and coordinating the activities of nearly 690,000 foreign subsidiaries around the globe.

The management and integration of such dispersed and often interdependent operations, necessitated by the search for global efficiencies, can only be achieved through the strategic deployment of information and communication technologies at subsidiary locations around the world. Common standards and global infrastructures within the MNC play a critical role in ensuring that subsidiary behavior and decision making remain consonant with overall corporate objectives. Such attempts at control and coordination, however, are often met with significant resistance from host country functional managers seeking to maintain a stable operating environment within their local branches. Corporate information systems (IS) managers can oftentimes find themselves in a position where they are required to leverage their influence at the headquarters to force subsidiaries to adhere to global standards. Resource dependence theory (RDT) argues that such efforts are made easier if subsidiary operations are reliant on services and technologies from an MNC's corporate IS operations.

RDT, first presented in Pfeffer and Salancik's 1978 book, *External Control of Organizations: A Resource Dependence Perspective,* has emerged as a powerful approach to explaining organizational behavior and interorganizational relationships.

Over the past three decades, Pfeffer and Salancik's work has been cited over 2,000 times and has been used as the basis to understand and interpret a wide variety of phenomena ranging from ownership issues in franchising to stakeholder influence on corporate strategies.

Despite the widespread acceptance of the theory, however, there has been a surprising dearth of empirical studies specifically attempting to test the validity of RDT. Indeed, Pfeffer and Salancik note that "there is a limited amount of empirical work explicitly testing resource dependence and its central tenets". This study attempts to address this research gap in the context of IS management in multinational organizations. Specifically, this research tests the validity of RDT in the context of headquarters—subsidiary IS operations in MNCs and addresses two questions. The first research question examines the relationship between resource dependence and level of control and coordination exerted by the headquarters IS management over subsidiary operations. Formally stated:

RQ1: Is the control and coordination exerted by an MNC headquarters over subsidiary IS operations influenced by the host country IS resource availability, dependence, and subsidiary strategic role?

The second research question examines the influence of the subsidiary-specific factors (strategic role, resource availability, and dependence) which determine the strategic relationship of the subsidiary and MNC headquarters, and the *types* of mechanisms used to enforce control and coordination.

RQ2: Does the strategic relationship influence the types of control and coordination mechanisms utilized to manage subsidiary IS operations?

1. The Research Model

This paper argues that, based on the findings and conclusions of prior studies, the resource-control-dependence scenario extends to the case of intra-organizational control and coordination in MNCs. Specifically, it is argued that under conditions where subsidiary IS management has only limited local access to resources needed to provide adequate technological infrastructure, it will depend on the parent company for the required resources. This resource dependency, along with the strategic role of the subsidiary, will significantly determine the nature of the *strategic relationship* between parent and subsidiary units in a given MNC. This strategic relationship will, in turn, influence the level of control and coordination (both formal and informal) exerted over the IS management of the subsidiary unit. It should be noted that both "strategic relationship" and "level of control and coordination" represent latent variables that are created as part of the analytical method used (canonical correlation analysis).

2. The Hypotheses

To test the validity of RDT in the context of IS management in MNCs, the relationship between level of control and coordination (FORMAL and INFORMAL), and three key variables (RESOURCE, DEPENDEN, and SROLE) are examined (Figure 4.1).

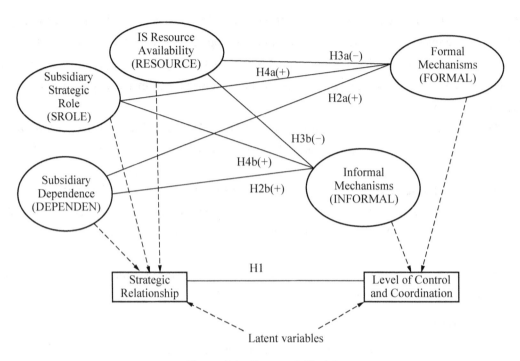

Figure 4.1　Research Model

(1) Level of Control and Coordination

As noted earlier, managers in MNCs must continually face the issue of the strategic integration of their operations in a variety of different host country environments. This integration is typically achieved through the careful manipulation of two types of mechanisms—formal and informal. Formal controls are those mechanisms that enforce a standard means of operating and reporting. Informal mechanisms of control and coordination are those that focus on fostering vertical and lateral communications within the organizational network and developing a consistent worldwide company culture. In this study, formal mechanisms (FORMAL) are operationalized as the level of usage of planning and standardization mechanisms imposed by the corporate headquarters. Informal mechanisms (INFORMAL) are operationalized as the level of use of coordination mechanisms such as personal contact, manager transfers, committees, task forces, conferences, and centralized training.

(2) IS Resource Availability

The growing trend toward global integration of value-added activities has emphasized the need for organizations to seek out greater information on the foreign environments in which they intend to operate. Makhija et al. write: "firms seek environments… where the appropriate skills, infrastructure and resources exist". In situations where such resources do not exist at the level and quality necessary for purposes of integration, the necessary skills and infrastructure must be sought from corporate headquarters. In this study, IS resource availability (RESOURCE) is measured in terms of the availability and quality of essential hardware, software, vendor support, and skilled IS personnel, in a given host country.

(3) Dependence

According to RDT, the adequacy of a country's IS and IS resources will play a role in determining the dependence of an MNC subsidiary on the headquarters for meeting necessary infrastructure requirements. In this paper, dependence (DEPENDEN) is measured as the perceived dependence of the subsidiary on corporate headquarters for essential hardware, software, vendor support, and skilled IS personnel.

(4) Strategic Role

As noted earlier, MNCs are internally differentiated with different subsidiaries playing a variety of strategic roles within the company's global network. The strategic role of the subsidiary unit is expected to significantly influence the strategic relationship between the corporate headquarters and the country unit, and hence, the types of control and coordination mechanisms used. This study utilizes the framework proposed by Gupta and Govindarajan and operationalizes subsidiary strategic role (SROLE) as the level of knowledge flows to and from the subsidiary to other units in the MNC network.

It is hypothesized that there is a significant relationship between the set of predictors of strategic relationship (RESOURCE, DEPENDEN, and SROLE) and the control and coordination set of variables (FORMAL and INFORMAL).

That is, *Hypothesis 1: The strategic relationship between a headquarters and subsidiary IS management operations is significantly associated with the use of formal and informal mechanisms of control and coordination.*

Further, with regard to dependence:

Hypothesis 2a: Subsidiaries exhibiting higher levels of dependence on IS resources from an MNC headquarters are associated with higher levels of usage of formal mechanisms of control and coordination.

Hypothesis 2b: Subsidiaries exhibiting higher levels of dependence on IS resources from an MNC headquarters are associated with higher levels of usage of informal mechanisms of control and coordination.

Also, with regard to the availability of IS resources:

Hypothesis 3a: Subsidiaries operating in countries with high availability of IS resources are associated with lower levels of usage of formal mechanisms of control and coordination.

Hypothesis 3b: Subsidiaries operating in countries with high availability of IS resources are associated with lower levels of usage of informal mechanisms of control and coordination.

Finally, with regard to the strategic role of a subsidiary, it is hypothesized that

Hypothesis 4a: Subsidiaries characterized by high knowledge flows with other subsidiaries are associated with higher levels of usage of formal mechanisms of control and coordination.

Hypothesis 4b: Subsidiaries characterized by high knowledge flows with other subsidiaries are associated with higher levels of usage of informal mechanisms of control and coordination.

3. Methodology

To statistically test the hypotheses suggested by the research model presented in the previous section, the study utilizes a linked-pair design in which a valid data point is defined as matched data collected from the headquarters of an MNC and from one of its subsidiary units. The data analyzed here was collected as part of a larger survey on the IS management function in MNCs.

(1) Data Collection

Two questionnaires were administered as part of the survey—a headquarters instrument to be completed by a senior IS manager at the corporate headquarters and a subsidiary instrument targeted at the senior IS manager at the subsidiary unit of the MNC.

An initial draft of the headquarters questionnaire was developed and discussed with a panel of expert academicians, which resulted in several revisions. The second draft of the headquarters instrument was pretested with the CIOs of seven large MNCs. Subsequent telephone interviews with three of the respondents indicated that no further changes were required to the instrument.

An initial draft of the subsidiary questionnaire was also developed and discussed with a panel of academic experts. After incorporating several revisions, a second draft of the subsidiary instrument was pretested by administering the questionnaire to two subsidiary IS managers—one in the United Kingdom and one in India. No revisions were required. Table 4-2 shows how each construct was operationalized.

The first attempt for obtaining a response from an MNC headquarters and (subsequently) a subsidiary was through standard postal services. Failing a mail response within two to three weeks, telephone calls were placed. For headquarters, the questionnaire was administered over the telephone. This was possible due to the shortness of the headquarters survey.

Table 4-3 provides the response rates for the survey. The final sample included responses from 54 headquarter–subsidiary surveys. Responses were received from 19 countries across six continents and a variety of industries. Table 4-4 presents the sample characteristics.

(2) Analysis and Results

In this study, canonical correlation analysis was conducted using the two coordination variables (FORMAL and INFORMAL) as predictors of the three independent variables (DEPENDEN, RESOURCE, and SROLE). CCA is a member of the multiple general linear hypothesis family of methods and is used to examine the relationship between two sets of variables. It is most appropriate when there are two or more interrelated dependent variables that need to be simultaneously evaluated against a set of independent variables. Like regular correlation, canonical correlation squared (R_c^2) is the percent of variance in the dependent set explained by the independent set along a given dimension. Thus, while traditional multiple regression models are used to examine one-to-many relationships, CCA is used for many-to-many relationships.

As indicated above, CCA is used when there are two or more correlated dependent variables (if there were no relationship between the criterion variables, then it would have been possible to separately regress each on the set of independent variables). In this case, a simple bivariate correlation analysis yields a Pearson coefficient of 0.592, significant at the $p=0.01$ level, suggesting that CCA would indeed be an appropriate analytical method to use in the study.

Table 4-2　Operationalization of Constructs

Construct	Variable	Operationalization
Formal mechanisms	FORMAL	Number of formal mechanisms. Based on aggregate value of responses to four items in subsidiary instrument
Informal mechanisms	INFORMAL	Number of informal mechanisms. Based on aggregate value of responses to seven scaled items in subsidiary instrument
Strategic role	SROLE	Part a subsidiary plays as a provider of goods, services, or information to other peer subsidiaries in the MNC based on Gupta and Govindarajan framework. Operationalized as level of knowledge flows. Aggregate value using responses to four items in subsidiary instrument
Host country IS resources	RESOURCE	The required hardware, software, vendor support, and IS personnel available to a subsidiary in the host country. Operationalized as single index based on availability and quality of above resources. Aggregate value of responses to eight scaled items in subsidiary instrument
Dependence	DEPENDEN	The extent to which a foreign subsidiary relies on the MNC headquarters for necessary IS resources. Operationalized as single index of dependence on MNC headquarters for hardware, software, vendor support, personnel, and using responses to five scaled items in subsidiary instrument, training, aggregate value

Table 4-3 Survey Response Rates

Number of headquarters questionnaires mailed	610
Number of envelopes returned to sender	43
Effective sample frame size	567
Number of responses received	72
Effective response rate for headquarters questionnaires (percent)	12.7
Subsidiary response rate	
Number mailed to subsidiaries (one per headquarters response received)	72
Number of subsidiary responses received	59
Number of nonusable responses	5
Number of usable responses	54
Effective response rate for subsidiaries (percent)	75

Table 4-4 Sample characteristics

MNC characteristic	Minimum	Maximum	Average
International experience (years)	8	100	41.2
Country exposure (number of countries in which operations exist)	2	150	29.4
International presence (number of foreign subsidiaries)	2	150	33.3
International employment (number of employees outside home country)	104	173,419	12,680

It should be noted that CCA will yield as many canonical functions as there are variables in the smaller of the two variable sets. Hence, for this model, the analysis resulted in two canonical functions (or roots) with squared canonical correlations of 0.217 (Root 1) and 0.012 (Root 2) for each successive function. Collectively, the full model across both functions is statistically significant using the Wilks's $\lambda=0.773$ criterion, $F(6, 98.00)=2.24$, $p < 0.05$. Thus, H1 is supported. Dimension reduction analysis shows that, while the full model (Functions 1 to 2) is significant, the second function (Function 2 alone) is not ($F(2, 50.00) = 0.303$, $p = 0.74$). Thus, only the first function is further analyzed in this study. Table 4-5 presents the results of the analysis and includes the standardized canonical coefficients for the first function, as well the structure coefficients.

Using the recommended minimum of a 0.3 cutoff correlation for acceptable loading, the standardized canonical coefficients (R_c) for the latent predictor variable indicate that all three dimensions (DEPENDEN, RESOURCE, and SROLE) are important contributors to the *strategic relationship* composite. Similarly, for the *level of coordination* set of criterion variables, both FORMAL and INFORMAL notably contribute to the composite. The squared structure coefficient (R_s^2) indicates that, in the strategic relationship set, DEPENDEN and SROLE explain 30.7 percent and 26.4 percent of the variance, respectively, while RESOURCE only explains 8.9 percent. With regard to level of coordination, both FORMAL and INFORMAL make noteworthy contributions, explaining 66.2 percent and 90.2 percent of the variance.

Each dependent variable was also regressed on the set of the independent variables to parse out individual effects. It should be noted that the strong codependence of RESOURCE and DEPENDEN would normally be cause for multicollinearity concerns. In this case, however, the variance inflation factors (VIFs) were well below the recommended limit of ten and the possibility of errors stemming from such a statistical phenomenon were deemed to be minimal. Tables 4-6 and 4-7 present the results of the regression run.

The results of the multiple regression analysis suggest that the level of usage of formal mechanisms of control and coordination are strongly correlated to DEPENDEN (H2a supported) and moderately so with SROLE ($p = 0.061$; H4a supported).

The relationship between RESOURCE and FORMAL was not significant (H3a not supported). The relationship between DEPENDEN and INFORMAL was, however, highly significant (H2b supported) while RESOURCE was also strongly related but not in the direction hypothesized (H3b not supported). The relationship between SROLE and INFORMAL was not significant (H4b not supported).

Table 4-5 Canonical Solution for Dependence, Resource Availability, and Strategic Role Predicting Level of Use of Formal and Informal Mechanisms

Variable	R_c	R_s	R_s^2
Strategic relationship			
DEPENDEN	−0.937	−0.554	0.307
RESOURCE	0.714	0.299	0.089
SROLE	0.520	−0.514	0.264
Level of coordination			
FORMAL	0.388	0.814	0.662
INFORMAL	0.720	0.950	0.902

Table 4-6 Regression Analysis for FORMAL

Covariate	Standard Coefficient	Covariate error	t-value	p
Dependent variable: FORMAL				
DEPENDEN	0.319	0.259	−2.135	0.038**
RESOURCE	0.244	0.314	1.633	0.109
SROLE	0.251	0.361	−1.920	0.061*

Notes: * significant at $p < 0.10$; ** significant at $p < 0.05$; *** significant at $p < 0.01$

Table 4-7 Regression Analysis for INFORMAL

Dependent variable: INFORMAL

Standard	Covariate	Coefficient error	t-value	p
DEPENDEN	0.43	0.183	−2.989	0.004***
RESOURCE	0.33	0.222	2.273	0.027**
SROLE	0.20	0.255	−1.581	0.120

Notes: * significant at $p < 0.10$; ** significant at $p < 0.05$; *** significant at $p < 0.01$

4. Discussion

The primary objective of this study was to test the validity of RDT in the context of global IS operations of an MNC. Although the overall model is significant, it is also interesting to note that the results suggest that the use of both formal and informal mechanisms are significantly and positively associated with the level of IS dependence a subsidiary has on its parent organization. Thus, as predicted by RDT, the greater the level of dependence, the greater the use of both formal and informal mechanisms of control. The results for resource availability, however, were more surprising. Based on the analysis, while there was no significant relationship between RESOURCE and FORMAL, the association between RESOURCE and INFORMAL was significant but not in the direction expected. The results suggest that the higher the availability of IS resources in the host country, the greater the level of use of informal mechanisms of control and coordination. This clearly runs counter to the expectations of RDT that argues that resource-rich environments would normally be less susceptible to headquarters control.

A possible explanation is that the availability of high-quality IS resources in a country environment may actually encourage a corporate headquarters to implement a variety of control and coordination mechanisms in a subsidiary and that it is in the best interest of the subsidiary to comply. One of the key weaknesses of RDT lies in the fact it does not adequately address issues of power imbalance and mutual dependence. Power imbalance is defined as the ratio of the power of a more powerful entity (such as a headquarters) to that of a less powerful one (such as a subsidiary). The fundamental tenets of RDT appear to hold when dealing with dyadic relationships characterized by high power imbalance. The influence of this imbalance can, however, be moderated by the mutual dependence of the actors. Mutual dependence refers to the existence of bilateral dependencies in the headquarters–subsidiary relationship. Given the global nature of competition, both the headquarters and subsidiaries may be damaged by failure to coordinate in the dyadic relationship (regardless of the lack of power imbalance stemming from subsidiaries' operating in a resource-rich environment). Alternatively, it is possible that, given the subsidiary has access to the technologies and personnel required to make complex integrative mechanisms feasible, such high-technology environments actually make the subsidiaries ideal locations for a global center of excellence and thus transform their strategic role into a critical one.

In turn, they become more important to control. While bridging or buffering strategies are often utilized to reduce dependence and susceptibility to external control, such an approach may be infeasible in organizational environments that seek high levels of IS integration. Subsidiaries operating in environments with limited IS resources may not have the skills or necessary technology available locally to make the use of control and coordination mechanisms possible. It is interesting to note that, while the use of informal mechanisms is significantly associated with IS resource availability, formal mechanisms are not. This may mean that the control and coordination of subsidiary IS operations where the subsidiary has sufficient access to the necessary IS resources (hence, low dependence on the parent) must be achieved through "softer" informal mechanisms, rather than the more heavy-handed formal mechanism of control. This receives some theoretical support when considering power imbalances and mutual dependence. In situations where there is high mutual dependence between the headquarters and subsidiary with little power imbalance (due to subsidiaries' operating in resource-rich environments), there is significant scope for the two actors to negotiate.

Excessive demands from one party (headquarters) in the shape of formal controls are likely to be less successful than "softer" informal mechanisms. Thus, while RDT may apply for formal mechanisms of control and coordination, it may not appropriately explain the use of informal mechanisms.

Given the overall research design and cross-sectional nature of the data collected for the study, however, it is not possible to definitively state that the quality and availability of IS resources influence the implementation of control and coordination mechanisms.

An alternative explanation is that the actual deployment and use of the mechanisms creates an IS environment in which the required resources and skills have been made available. That is, the use of the integrative mechanisms *creates* the necessary IS environment. Further research would be required to make a determination.

The seeming lack of significance of strategic role in determining the use of control and coordination mechanisms is also interesting. While there was a moderately significant ($p = 0.061$) relationship between a subsidiary unit's strategic role and the use of formal mechanisms, there was none in the case of informal mechanisms. This suggests that MNCs still rely more on the use of standardization and similar mechanisms that force a particular subsidiary behavior for those units perceived as critical to global operations rather than facilitating coordination through contacts and communication.

5. Limitations

In any international field study involving multiple countries and several industries, there are a number of limitations that place bounds on the external validity of the findings. While these limitations do not negate the veracity of the results, it is important to acknowledge them so that the findings may be interpreted in the context in which the research was designed and the data collected.

First, there is a significant volume of empirical IS research that has been published that looks at IS issues in purely domestic organizations. There is a paucity, however, of similar research in the context of technology management in MNCs. This is not surprising, given the difficulty and expense involved in conducting such studies. The unfortunate consequence of this fact is that there is a limited theoretical base in IS literature to use as a foundation for relevant research models. It becomes necessary, therefore, to extrapolate the findings of research conducted in many other disciplines of management to the research model used here. Thus, the research model developed here is based on prior studies conducted at the overall organization level, rather than at the level of the IS function.

Second, the sample size of 54 data points is relatively small. Survey research is a common means of collecting data. Many respondents indicated that they were deluged by requests for participation in studies and had established company policies that prevented them from responding. Although the sample size is cause for some concern, it meets the rule-of-thumb minimum of five data points per independent variable.

Finally, the generalizability of the findings is always a problem for empirical studies drawing on a limited sample. Several companies that did not respond were contacted by telephone to assess the possibility of a nonresponse bias. The IS managers at these organizations indicated that the study was relevant to them but they did not have the time to complete the questionnaire. It is also acknowledged that, while the sampling of MNC headquarters to be included in the study was random, the selection of subsidiaries was not. Given that the research design called for headquarters respondents to identify subsidiaries to be contacted, it is possible that the subsidiary sample may reflect some bias. For example, headquarters respondents may have selected subsidiaries they communicated with most frequently. The possible implication of such a selection bias would be that the subsidiary units represented in the sample are too similar and offer insufficient variance for appropriate analysis. While the study asked that headquarters managers identify various types of subsidiaries, this was not always done. The results of the study must be interpreted in this context. Every attempt was made, however, to ensure the subsidiary sample was as representative as possible.

6. Conclusion

Resource dependence theory has long been used to explain the relationship between parent and subsidiary units in large organizations. This paper attempted to test the validity of the theory in the context of IS management in subsidiary units of multinational corporations. While the theory holds up well in the case of dependence, the expected relationship with IS resource availability was not observed. Although there was a significant relationship with the use of informal mechanisms of control and coordination, it was in the opposite direction to what was expected. This suggests that the type of mechanism (formal or informal) used is an important factor when examining the resource-control issue. Further research is needed to examine the influence of the specific types of control mechanisms and when they are most effective.

Part 4 Reading Comprehension 阅读理解

Passage 1 A Smuggling Syndicate 走私辛迪加

The smuggler in many ways is just another international businessman and his turnover would do credit to many international corporations. His business happens to be illegal and risky, but look at the stakes involved: $5 billion worth of heroin smuggled into the United States each year, and $1.5 billion in gold passing annually along smuggling pipelines to India and Indonesia, to France and Morocco, to Brazil and Turkey. Perhaps half of all the watches made in Switzerland reach their eventual wearers by some back door. Most of this illicit trade is carried on with all the efficiency of any multinational company. Entirely legitimate businesses, such as a travel bureau or an import-export agency, are also often fronts for smuggling organizations. One of the world's largest gold smugglers also owned and operated the franchise for a leading make of British cars in a small Middle Eastern country. He made a good profit from both activities.

A smuggling syndicate operates much like any other business. The boss is really a chief executive. He makes all the plans, establishes international contacts, and thinks up the smuggling routes and method but remains aloof from actual operations. He is aided by a handful of managers looking after such specialties as financing, travel (one reason why many smuggling syndicates find it handy to have their own travel agency), the bribing of airline or customs officials, and recruitment of couriers, or mules as they are called. There may also be someone in charge of local arrangements in the countries to which the smuggled goods is going.

Another similarity between legitimate business and its illegal counterpart is price fluctuation. Just as the prices of products traded legally vary with quality and market conditions such as supply and demand, so do the prices of goods go up and down in the smuggling trade. Consider the price of drugs. Heroin and cannabis, in whatever form or by whatever name, cone in several grades, each with a going price. The wholesale price at which big dealers sell to big dealers is less than the street price. When the authorities are successful in reducing the supply buy seizures, the price of all grades rises.

1. The main idea for this passage is (   ).

   [A] the Comparison between legitimate business and its illegal counterpart

   [B] the similarities between legitimate business and smuggling

   [C] smugglers may make great profit from both activities

   [D] the boss in smuggling syndicate is a chief executive

2. When is the price going down? (   )

   [A] The quality of the foods and market condition are not very well

   [B] The quality of goods and market condition vary

   [C] Unbalance between supply and demand

   [D] The price of other goods fluctuates

3. It can be inferred that a smuggler (   ).

   [A] may make plan and establish international contacts

   [B] is a real boss

   [C] may make money in different ways

   [D] may sell other goods

4. One of the best ways smugglers usually take is (   ).

   [A] to set up multinational companies

   [B] to engage in illegal businesses only

   [C] to make legitimate businesses as fronts for smuggling organizations

   [D] to make good profits from both activities

Passage 2 FDI and Business Acquisitions 直接投资与并购

The following paragraphs are given in a wrong order. For Questions 1-5, you are required to reorganize these paragraphs into a coherent text by choosing from the list A-G to fill in each numbered box. The first and the last paragraphs have been placed for you in Boxes.

[A] Foremost on every potential buyer's list of concerns is debt. The average South Korean Company is leveraged four times over its equity, which is why so many are desperate to liquidate assets. But because Korea's currency lost half its value last year, many Korean executives believe—mistakenly—that foreign buyers will find their wares attractive in spite of their debts, analysts says.

Unit 4
International Cooperation and Transnational Corporation 国际合作与跨国公司

[B] Despite such aversion to foreign ownership, some deals are going through. Directors of Bank of Asia are believed to have approved the sale of a stake in their midsize bank to Dutch bank ABN-Amro. For the Bank of Thailand, the central bank, the ABN-Amro deal will send a much needed signal that the country is welcoming foreign capital.

[C] "The attitude of Koreans is that only foreigners will pay the price they are as king," says Daniel Harwood of ABN-Amro Asia in Seoul. But foreigners are looking at these business and saying "How can I make a profit," not "Oh, it's cheap, and I'll buy it." No one will take over these companies unless they can restructure.

[D] Survival is usually uppermost in the minds of companies with their backs to the wall, even if that entails being reduced to a minority stake. In Thailand, however, most ailing companies seem loathe to admit that their conditions may be fatal. "They aren't realistic," says Henry Conell, Goldman Sachs' Hong Kong based partner in charge of direct investment in Asia. "Nobody is about to say to them, you will be gone."

[E] In south Korea, interest from foreigners has focused more on the country's manufacturers. But, the number of actual purchases, like those in Thailand, is small. In any event, big ticket cross border mergers and acquisitions are bound to take time. Indeed, analysts say the main reason for the dearth of deals so far is due to diligence: foreign investors must thoroughly familiarize themselves with companies they might buy. "You can't do this stuff overnight," says a senior official at a large Western bank in Seoul.

[F] Still, the number of deals is growing by the day. On February 19, Samsung Heavy Industries simultaneously sold its excavator division to Sweden's Volvo Construction Equipment and its forklift operation to the United States' Clark Martirial Handling. Earlier, the chemical giant Hanwha group sold two affiliates to its Japanese and German partners. Despite the slow start, no one doubts that the bargains at Korea Inc. are for real.

[G] Thai businesses' unwillingness to sell hasn't been helped by the government's own ambivalence. While Finance Minister Tarrin Nimmanahaeminda is committed to attracting foreign money to Thailand, Deputy Prime Minister SupachaiPanitchpakdi seems less so. "We don't want foreign firms to come and buy out our businesses. We want them to come, buy shares, and operate firms   and sell them after making profits." he told the local media recently. "This will give Thais a chance to buy them back."

Order:

D→   1(　)→   2(　)→   3(　)→   4(　)→   5(　)→   F

Part 5 课 文 注 释

1. Joint ownership of an operation in which at least one of the partners is foreign based.

翻译：合资企业将用来指一种经营的共同所有权，合伙者中至少有一方是外方。

2. Management may wish to reinvest earnings while the majority of the board may wish earnings distributed as dividends.

翻译：管理层可能希望将盈利进行再投资，而董事会大多数成员则可能希望将盈利作为红利予以分配。

3. Many joint ventures emerge as matters of necessity: that is, no single firm is willing to assume the risks entailed, while a consortium of firms is. Large, capital-intensive, long-lived investments are natural candidates for the joint-venture.

翻译：很多合资企业的出现是很必要的，这就是说，没有单独的一家企业愿意承担出现的风险，但是由于企业联合财团是大型的，资本密集和长期投资就自然地成为合资企业的选择对象。

4. However, increasingly, joint ventures are an extension of nationalism and are undertaken as a condition of entry rather than as a permissive arrangement between firms.

翻译：然而合资企业逐渐成为民族主义的产物，答应办合资企业成为进入(东道国) 的一个条件，而不是作为企业之间同意的协议。

5. As noted, the joint venture can pose problems, especially if it is an enforced marriage of partners. For many ventures in small countries, it is difficult to find a suitable local partner, that is, one with sufficient capital and know-how to be able to contribute to the partnership.

翻译：正如所提到的，合资企业可能会产生一些问题，特别是在合作者被强迫合作的情况下，小国家的很多企业很难找到合适的合作伙伴，即一个能够给合作者带来足够资金和技术的伙伴。

6. The transnational enterprises (TNEs) play a central role in the transfer of technology and the rate of technological diffusion.

翻译：跨国公司在技术转让和技术扩散的速度中起着关键作用。

7. The dominant channel of transfer is through world trade. Direct forms of transfer include licenses, patents, sale of technological know-how, and direct investment. Firms in the industrialized countries increasingly use a combination of these channels to gain new technological expertise.

翻译：转让的主要渠道是通过国际贸易。转让的直接形式有许可证、专利、技术诀窍的销售和直接投资。工业化国家的企业正日益将这些渠道结合起来以获得新的技术知识。

International Cooperation and Transnational Corporation 国际合作与跨国公司

8. Meanwhile, the politics of economic cooperation between the Western market economics and the Eastern, centralized economies that has prevailed for the past two decades has provided opportunities for trade between these two groups, and along with the trade has come the transfer of technology。

翻译：同时，在过去20年中，西方市场经济国家和东方中央经济国家之间的经济合作政策占了主导地位，这为两个集团之间的贸易提供了机会，在进行贸易的同时也展开了技术转让。

9. Technological transfers through trade range from simple products to the highly sophisticated technological systems normally traded between firms in the industrialized countries.

翻译：通过贸易进行的技术转让，涉及从工业化国家企业之间通常所进行交易的一般产品到高度精密的成套技术设备。

10. The rate of diffusion varies with the type of technology and is determined by the degree of difficulty of transfer. The costs of transferring the technology increase with the difficulty.

翻译：技术由于类型的不同，扩散的速度也不同，它由转让的难度所决定。技术转让的难度越大成本越高。

11. General technology involves information that is common to an industry or trade and represents the general state of technological knowledge in the industry or trade.

翻译：一般技术是某工业或行业共同所有的知识，代表着该工业和行业的一般技术知识状况。

12. Firm-specific technology refers to technology specific to a particular firm's experience, activities, and know-how, but not attributable to any specific item the firm products.

翻译：企业特有技术是指某一公司所特有的经验、活动和技术诀窍，并非指和该公司所生产的某一特定产品相关。

13. System-Specific technology concerns the technology used in the production of a production of a product by all manufacturers within the industry.

翻译：成套设备特有技术是指某工业中所有制造商在生产某一产品时所采用的技术。

14. Hence, much of the changing shape of the global economic system is sculptured by the TNC through its decisions to invest or not to invest in particular geographical locations.

翻译：所以全球经济机制的转型在很大程度上由跨国公司决定是否在某些特定地区投资而定。

15. One way of defining a transnational is in terms of its ownership of overseas assets and activities, where such ownership confers control over the overseas operation.

翻译：一种界定跨国公司的办法是依据它是否拥有海外公司资产以及海外业务，而这种所有权使其能控制海外公司经营活动。

16. A transnational is the means of co-coordinating production from one center of strategic decision making when this co-coordinating takes a firm across national boundaries.

翻译：跨国公司是一种战略决策中心进行调节的手段，这种协调使公司跨越国界。

17. It is, therefore, not subject to external market prices but to the internal decisions of TNCs.

翻译：所以这种贸易不是受制于外部市场价格，而是受制于跨国公司内部决策。

18. In effect, international trade in manufactured goods looks less and less like the trade of basic economic models in which buyers and sellers interact freely with one another (in reasonably competitive markets) to establish the volume and prices of traded goods.

翻译：事实上，制造品的国际贸易运作已经摆脱了买卖双方在竞争市场中共同确定贸易量和贸易价格的基本经济模式。

19. Even so, the degree of foreign involvement by these giant firms is extremely high. In addition, during the postwar period the leading TNCs have become increasingly global in their production.

翻译：即便如此，这些巨人公司在海外生产经营的跨国性程度极高，而且战后的这段时间里，主要跨国公司的经营活动已经日益全球化。

20. The smuggler in many ways is just another international businessman and his turnover would do credit to many international corporations.

翻译：走私者在许多方面就像一个国际商人，而他的营业额确为许多国际公司增光。

Part 6　词汇及扩展

joint venture 合资企业
capital intensive 资本密集型
labor intensive 劳动密集型
technology intensive 技术密集型
parcel out 分为数份
equity 股票，证券
to shy away 避开
to engage in 从事于
market-oriented economies 市场经济国家
central planned economies 中央计划经济国家

International Cooperation and Transnational Corporation 国际合作与跨国公司

technological diffusion 技术扩散
advanced system 先进的成套设备
parent company 母公司
subsidiary 子公司
transnational corporations 跨国公司
multinational corporation 多国公司
global corporation/international corporation 国际公司
technological and organizational expertise 技术和管理专长
overseas assets 海外资产
coordinating production 统筹生产
equity relationship 产权关系
disproportionate 不匀称的，不均衡的
intra-firm 公司内部的
basic economic models 基本经济模式
affiliate 子公司，分支机构
nation-states 民族国家
direct investment aboard 对外直接投资
transnationality 跨国性
devaluation 贬值
revaluation 升值
trade deficit 贸易赤字
equilibrium 均衡，平衡
OECD (Organization for Economic Co-operation and Development) 经济合作与发展组织
monopoly 垄断
convertible 可兑换的
SEZs (Special Economic Zones) 经济特区
FIEs (Foreign-invested Enterprise) 外商直接投资企业
FDI (Foreign Direct Investment) 外商直接投资
turnover 营业额
do credit to 为某人/某物增光
stake 下在投机生意上的股本，赌注
smuggling pipeline 走私线路
speciality 专业部门，公司
recruit 招募，添补(新兵)

Part 7 网络学习资源

1. 有关外商直接投资的资料有联合国出版的《世界投资报告》(年报)、经合组织出版的《国际投资统计年报》和美国经济分析局每年 7-8 月份出版的《美国商业概览》，相关网址为：

http://www.unctad.org/en/docs

http://www.oecd.org

http://bea.doc.gov/bea/di1.htm

2. 关于工业国家财政和货币政策及其效果的数据可以参见以下机构的网址：国际清算银行(BIS)、经合组织(OECD) 以及美国国家经济研究局(NBER)。其网址分别是：

http://www.bis.org

http://www.oecd.org

http://www.nber.org

Unit 5　International Marketing and Management
国际营销与管理

Part 1　Intensive Reading　精读

Passage 1　International Marketing 国际市场营销

The term international marketing refers to exchanges across national boundaries for the satisfaction of human needs and wants. The extent of firm's involvement abroad is a function of its commitment to the pursuit of foreign markets. A firm's overseas involvement may fall into several categories.

(1) Domestic: Operate exclusively within a single country.

(2) Regional exporter: Operate within a geographically defined region that crosses national boundaries. Markets served are economically and culturally homogeneous. If activity occurs outside the home region, it is opportunistic.

(3) Exporter: Run operations from a central office in the home region, exporting finished goods to a variety of countries; some marketing, sales, and distribution outside the home region.

(4) International: Region operations are somewhat autonomous, but key decisions are made and coordinated from the central office in the home region. Manufacturing and assembly, marketing, and sales are decentralized beyond the home region. Both finished goods and intermediate products are exported outside the home region.

(5) International to global: Run independent and mainly self-sufficient subsidiaries in a range of countries. While some key functions (R&D, sourcing, financing) are decentralized, the home region is still the primary base for many functions.

(6) Global: Highly decentralized organization operating across a broad range of countries. No geographic area (including the home region) is assumed a priority to be the primary base for any functional area. Each function including R&D, sourcing, man-most suitable for that function.

Typically, the journey begins at home. Companies operating exclusively within a single country reach the limits to grow in their home market and face the need to expand to achieve further growth. The time that it takes to reach this outer growth limit depends almost entirely on the size of the home market. Thus, North American companies will take longer to reach the outer limit than companies in Singapore, South Korea and Japan, whose home markets are substantially smaller and provide less room to grow. Once the domestic barrier is reached, companies evolve into an export modality, either on a limited, regional basis where markets are still economically and culturally homogeneous, or on a broader basis where finished goods are exported to a variety of countries. Regional exporters companies continue to run operations from a central office in the home markets, though some marketing, sales, and distribution functions begin to crop up elsewhere.

As companies become more successful in their export operations, they reach that critical point where the need to achieve greater proximity to overseas markets becomes paramount. At this point, such companies begin to replicate their business systems in new markets by creating relatively autonomous regional operations. Manufacturing and assembly, marketing, and sales are decentralized and both finished goods and system intermediate products are exported outside the home region, but key decisions are made, or at least coordinate, by a head office in the home region. Companies that have reached this stage of evolution may be characterized as international companies. *The replication of a company's business system in various locations around the world does not, however, represent a long-term formula for profitable growth and, ultimately, international companies face the need to optimize their business globally by adopting a global mode of operation.* For global companies, no one geographic area is assumed to be the primary base for any function-research and development, sourcing, and manufacturing are situated in the most suitable locations worldwide.

The basic nature of marketing does not change from domestic to international marketing, but marketing outside national boundaries poses special problems. International marketing, unlike domestic marketing, requires operating simultaneously in more than one kind of environment, coordinating these operations, and using the experience gained in one country for making decisions in another country. The demands are tough and the stakes are high. International markets not only must be sensitive to different marketing environments internationally, but also must be able to balance marketing moves worldwide to seek optimum results for the company.

The impact of environment on international business can be illustrated by the watch industry. New technology, falling trade barriers, and changing cost relationships have affected the competitive patterns of the industry worldwide. Only companies with global perspective are operating successfully. A new world companies sell world products to increasingly brand-conscious consumers. This multinationalization of the watch industry has made four producers—Switzerland, Japan, Hong Kong SAR of China, and the U.S. —dominate the scene by emphasizing brand names. Manufacturing operations are specialized by country according to costs of specific processes, components, and subassemblies.

Unit 5 International Marketing and Management 国际营销与管理

To successfully compete globally, rather than simply operate domestically, companies should emphasize: ①*Global configuration of marketing activities (i.e., where activities such as new product development, advertising, sales promotion, channel selection, marketing research, and other functions should be performed);* ②*Global coordination of marketing activities (i.e., how global marketing activities performed in different countries should be coordinated); and* ③*linkage of marketing activities (i.e., how marketing activities should be linked with other activities of the firm).*

Many marketing activities, unlike those in other functional areas, must be dispersed in each host country to make an adequate response to the local environment. Not all marketing activities need to be performed on a dispersed basis, however. In many cases, competitive advantage is gained, in the form of lower cost or enhanced differentiation, if selected activities are performed centrally as a result of technological changes, buyer shifts, and evolution of marketing media. These activities include production of promotional materials, sales force and service support organization training, and advertising. Further international marketing activities dispersed in different countries should be properly coordinated to gain competitive advantages. *Such coordination can be achieved by:* ①*performing marketing activities using similar method across countries;* ②*transferring marketing know-how and skills from country to country;* ③*sequencing marketing programs across countries;* ④*integrating the efforts of varies marketing groups in different countries.*

Finally, a global view of international marketing permits linking marketing to upstream and support activities of the firm, which could lead to advantages in varies ways. *For example, marketing can unlock economies scale and learning in production and/or R&D by* ①*supporting the development of universal products by providing the information necessary to develop a physical product design that can be sold worldwide;* ②*creating demand for more universal products even if historical demand has been for more varied products in different countries;* ③*identifying and penetrating segments in many countries to allow the sale of universal products, and* ④*providing services and/or local accessories that effectively tailor the standard physical product to the local needs.*

Passage 2 International Marketing Communications 综合营销沟通

As integrated marketing becomes more and more the rule in agencies and companies, the need for communications cross-training — to learn different skills of marketing, advertising, sales promotion, and public relations becomes a requirement for all communicators.

Integrated marketing means approaching communications issues from the customer's perspective. Consumers don't separate promotional material or newspaper advertising or community responsiveness into separate compartments. They lump everything together to make judgments about services and organizations.

Integrated marketing expert Mitch Kozikowski lists six maxims that can guide public relations professionals through the communications cross-training process.

(1) Integrated marketing communication is not about ads, direct mail pieces, or public relations projects. It is about understanding the customer and what the consumer actually responds to.

(2) Organizations can't succeed without good relationships with their publics. Organizations need relationships with their customers that go beyond the pure selling of a product or service. They need to build relationships. As the world becomes more competitive in everything from health care to auto repair, from selling insurance to selling cereal, relationship building becomes more critical.

(3) Integrated marketing communications requires collaboration on strategy, not just on execution. This means that the entire communications function must be part of the launch of a product, service, campaign, or issue from its inception.

(4) Strategic plans must be clear on the role that each discipline is to play in solving the problem. The roles of advertising, marketing, and public relations are different. None can do everything by itself. Therefore, although advertising might control the message and marketing and product promotion might provide support, it is public relations that should provide credibility for the product and, even more important, for the organization.

(5) Public relations are about relationships. Public relations professionals can become proprietors of integrated marketing communications. Because the essence of public relation is building relationships between an institution and its publics, public relations professionals, perhaps more than any other, should lead the integrated marketing initiative. Public relations professionals have long understand the importance of the two-way communication that builds strong relationships with customers and others. Such an understanding is pivotal to the successful rendering of integrated marketing communications.

(6) To be players in integrated marketing communications, public relations professionals need to practice more than the craft of public relations. Simply stated, for public relations people must expand their horizons, increase their knowledge of other disciplinary skills building.

Element of public relations—among them product publicity, special events, spokesman-ship, and similar activities—can enhance a marketing effort. A new discipline—marketing communications—has emerged that uses many of the techniques of public relations.

Marketing, literally defined, is the selling of a service or product through pricing, distribution, and promotion. Public relations, liberally defined, is the marketing of an organization. Most organizations now realize that public relations can play an expanded role in marketing.

Unit 5 International Marketing and Management 国际营销与管理

Stated another way, although the practice of marketing creates and maintains a market for products and services, and the practice of public relations creates and maintains a hospitable environment in which the organization may operate, marketing success can be nullified by the social and political forces public relations is designed to confront—and thus the interrelationship of the two disciplines.

In the past, marketers treated public relations as an ancillary part of the marketing mix. They were concerned primarily with making sure that their products met the needs and desires of customers and were priced competitively, distributed widely, and promoted heavily through advertising and merchandising. Gradually, however, these traditional notions among marketers began to change for several reasons.

(1) Consumer protests about both product value and safety and government scrutiny of the truth of product demands began to shake historical views of marketing.

(2) Product recalls from automobiles to tuna fish, generated recurring headlines.

(3) Ingredient scares began to occur regularly.

(4) Advertisers were asked how their products answer social needs and civic responsibilities.

(5) Rumors about particular companies—from fast-food firms to pop rock manufacturers—spread in brushfire manner.

(6) General image problems of certain companies and industries— from oil to banking—were fanned by a continuous blaze of media criticism.

The next impact of all this was that even though a company's products were still important, customers began to consider a firm's policies and practices on everything from air and water pollution to minority hiring.

Passage 3 Public Relations and the Net 公共关系和网络

In public relations, as in other fields, nothing is more important, as the world enters the twenty-first century, than mastering the interactive workplace: cyberspace, the Internet, the World Wide Web. The computer apparently rules, and all else seems to pale by comparison.

Although the computer has unleashed tremendous potential power for public relations and other communications disciplines, particularly in the areas of research and access to information, its promise has thus far exceeded its payoff. By the end of the 1990s, there were many signs that the early Web bloom was off the rose.

(1) America Online (AOL), the nation's largest online provider, closed down its Global Network Navigator operations, the first commercial web site, in 1996 after failing to make it work.

CMP Publications slashed the staff of its Web magazine, also started with great fanfare, from 200 workers to 65.

That's the discouraging news. The better news is that no area of public relations work is "hotter" in the new millennium than the development of Web sites, Intranet operations, and the general harness of the web to communicate with target publics. Although the wonders of the Web are only evolving, attention to the computer and what it can provide the public relations practitioner are the topics that dominate discussion.

(2) Almost one in four Americans adults—nearly 50 million people—have used the Internet. Another 12 million annually take the Internet plunge.

More than half log on from home and about 30 percents are in the 25-to-34-year-old population, the fastest growing segment of the on-line population. Although women comprise 45 percent of users, males are heavier Internet user by three-to-one. Nearly half of all users in this early stage of Web development rate their overall on-line satisfaction as "very good" or "excellent".

The burgeoning growth of the World Wide Web is not with its downside. Although the Internet increases in popularity every day, it is bogged down — gridlocked — by too many users, contributing a continuous and unrestrained stream of communication, much labeled "shovelware", or, literally translated, unadulterated garbage. The number of pages on the Web has mushroomed from a few thousand in 1992 to an estimated 50 million. In terms of how clogged it is, government scientists have warned that the Internet is in a "dangerous state". The danger lies largely in the inverse correlation between volume of information available compared to that which is useful.

(3) *Although traffic on the world's computer network is booming, most firms that provide the Net's infrastructure — the telecommunications lines and access services— lose money in the business.* Some of the nation's largest advertising agencies, quick to set up "interactive divisions", have either cut them back or abandoned them entirely. The "hope" for the future is that as Web usage continues to grow, higher volume will bring increased profitability.

Nonetheless, despite its detractions and its early fits and starts, the fact is that the World Wide Web is but in its infancy. There is no question that in the twenty-first century, the Internet will become an increasing powerful communications vehicle and a growing important vehicle for public relations practitioners.

Compared to some other industries, such as stock brokerage and advertising, public relations professionals have been relatively slow to use the Internet to advance their own messages and those of their clients. Nonetheless, for three reasons in particular, use of the Net by public relations practitioners inevitably will grow in the future.

First, the demand to be educated versus being sold. Today's consumers are smarter, better

International Marketing and Management 国际营销与管理 Unit 5

educated, and more media savvy. They know when they are being hustled by self-promoters and con artists. So communications programs must be grounded in education-based information, rather than blatant promotion. The Net is perhaps the world's greatest potential repository of such information.

Second, the need for real-time performance. The world is moving quickly. Everything happens instantaneously, in real-time. Public relations professionals can use this to their advantage to structure their information to respond instantly to emerging issues and market change.

Third, the need for customization. There used to be three primary television networks. Today, there are more than 500 television channels. Today's consumers expect more focused, targeted, one-on-one communications relationships.

Such is the promise of the Internet to the practice of public relations. In terms of the broad use of cyberspace by public relations professionals, electronic mail or e-mail is probably the most pervasive internal mechanism. In a growing number of organizations, e-mail, delivered on-line and immediately, has replaced traditional print publications and the even more recent fax technology as a rapid delivery information vehicle. An outgrowth of e-mail—Internets or intranets are another growing phenomenon.

Another rapidly expanding use of the Net by public relations professionals is the creation and maintenance of Web sites to profile companies, promote produces, or position issues. Federal Express sets two goals for its Web site: To do business and to provide up-to-date unfiltered news.

Part 2   Extensive Reading   泛读

Passage 1   International Marketing Planning and Strategy 国际营销计划与策略

The essence of international marketing management is the development of appropriate objective, strategies, and plans that culminate in the successful realization of foreign marketing opportunities. The world marketplace is marked by accelerating change, requiring explicit statements of objectives and strategies.

Business across national boundaries became a dominant factor in world commerce after World War II. Today, for a number of U.S. companies, as well as for many non-U.S. multinationals sales and/or revenues from overseas exceed domestic business. The international marketplace is changing fast. In 1960s, U.S. corporations had an edge in many ways, but no longer. In such markets as automobiles, steel, watches, textile goods, and electrical equipment, there is fierce competition. In addition to multinational enterprises from Europe and Japan, corporations belonging to developing nations, such as South Korea, China, Brazil, and India, are increasingly participating in world markets, giving rise to new forms of competition.

Currently, MNCs are expanding at a rate of more than 10 percent a year, or twice the growth rate for gross world product. The prospect is that the business organizations will become even more important in the future. According to the projections of knowledgeable economists based on present trends, in the year 2000, the economy of the world will be more than half internationalized.

Although markets overseas are changing and competition increasing, international markets offer attractive opportunities. As a matter of fact, markets across national boundaries frequently offer higher rates of return than domestic markets. However, to make a mark in the international arena, a company needs to define its objectives clearly, choosing appropriate strategies, and develop adequate plans to implement the chosen strategies.

Planning practices for multinational markets are far behind those for domestic markets. This is particularly true of strategic planning. Theoretically, international marketing planning and strategy should involve both subsidiary and headquarters management. Further, planning should focus on operational matters as well as strategic issues. Currently, however, most marketing planning among MNCs is operational and short-term. In a great many corporations, the effort amounts to a set of financial figures extrapolated for the next four to six quarters. In some cases, the plan is put together by headquarters staff with meager inputs from the subsidiary. In some corporations, however, the planning task is entirely delegated to subsidiary management. In the latter case, the headquarters' view is skimpy and only ritualistic.

The challenge of successfully competing in the international field in the future will force corporations to become more systematic in planning efforts. Every industry must look ahead—1 year, 5 years, 10 years—and plan for: ①the future political, social, and economic environment; ②the evolution of that particular industry; and ③how the industry must change to meet the problems and opportunities it judges it will face.

Essentially, marketing planning at the subsidiary level is short-term planning related to the next 12 to15 months and not strategic planning, which usually has a long-run focus. A subsidiary's planning efforts should be duly coordinated with those at headquarters. Characteristically, it should be from the bottom-up and should take into account the environmental realities surrounding its products/markets. In this effort, the parent corporation plays two roles. *The first role involves facilitating linkage between corporate and subsidiary perspectives. This amounts to providing corporate-wide perspectives relative to its overall mission and direction, both generally and with reference to the subsidiary/country market. The second role includes establishing a worldwide* planning system. Such a system is achieved by developing planning procedures and communicating them to subsidiaries. An additional role that corporate headquarters must perform is to serve as a catalyst in creating a planning culture among the subsidiary executives.

At headquarters, marketing planning focuses on coordination and approval of plans submitted by subsidiaries, as well as formulation of corporate-wide strategy. The strategy formulation in international business reflects not only the domestic experience of the company, but also management's orientation toward multinational business. There are usually three management orientations: ethnocentrism, polycentrism, and geocentrism. A company with a geocentric perspective tends to look at world markets as a whole, with no demarcation between domestic and international business. Its strategic focus is global. However, an executive with an ethnocentric orientation views international business as secondary, a place to dispose of "surplus" products left over after fulfilling domestic demand.

Passage 2   E-commercial 电子商务

1. Characters of Online Commerce

An online commerce customer faces mediation in every element and at every stage of the commerce transaction. Customers can't see the merchant, only the merchant's website; they can't touch the merchandise, they can only see a representation; they can't wander a store and speak with employees, they can only browse HTML pages, read FAQs, and fire off email to nameless customer service mailboxes; they can't explore the store's shelves and product space, they can only search a digital catalog. A customer at an online commerce site lacks the concrete cues to comfortably assess the trustworthiness of the site, and so must rely on new kinds of cues. The problem for the online customer is that the web is new—to a large sector of the online audience—and online commerce seems like a step into an unknown experience.

2. "Buy From Us"

The basic goal of a commerce site is to sell something, a product or a service; even if the company launching a commerce site has other goals, such as establishing an online presence, a commerce web site is a place for selling. Commerce sites use some powerful tools and techniques—including merchandising, advertising, reviews—to focus the "buy from us" message, make it stronger, and make it more attractive to the user.

As with any communicative transaction, the audience must build themselves an understanding of the meaning of the message. A user will follow various schemas for relationship mapping, including one for commerce. A user will pick up explicit cues from a commerce site, such as the product types for sale, prices, the purchasing/ordering track, maybe the scope of selection; these cues fill in the message "buy from us". The user also picks up implicit cues, often without realizing it, and it is to these implicit messages that commerce sites should pay particular attention.

If a commerce site's base message is "buy from us", then the site must take great care to avoid undoing that message inadvertently through contradictory messages or behavior. For example, a commerce site with prominent exit links on major pages is telling the user that they are welcome to leave the site; if you make it more interesting for a user to explorer another site, your message is more accurately "bye bye" than "buy from us". For another example, a commerce site that doesn't have an "add to cart" link next to products displayed on major pages, instead forcing users to navigate deep into the site to product detail pages, is making the buying process harder for user…a contradiction of the crucial "buy from us" message.

Commerce sites that are hard to reach because of access delays aren't crying "buy from us" effectively. A site that limits accessibility, either through the requirement of specific browsers, or the use of non-standard code, or even through an over-reliance on graphics, is diluting the audience of the message.

Remember that the user refers to three rough categories of information when making up his or her mind about your commerce site as a place worth buying from.

(1) Judgement of your site.

(2) Judgement of the company behind the site.

(3) Feelings and impressions that may be operating on a subconscious level.

The user relies on information gleaned not just from your obvious message but from their impression of your site, and by extension from their impression of the company behind the site. Users will look at a site and wonder about the decisions that led to the features and problems they see, and a bad impression derived from a user judgment is very difficult to undo.

3. "Trust Us"

If the basic message of any commerce site is "buy from us", the higher-level message—the metamessage—is "trust us". Users are unlikely to purchase from a site unless they are satisfied that the site is trustworthy. As with a user's perception of the simpler message "buy from us", users process multiple explicit and implicit cues when assessing a site's trustworthiness, but trust can be a tougher sell.

Every commerce web site has at least two core messages: at the most basic level, the user encounters the message "buy from us", while at a higher level the user faces the message "trust us". A commerce site may also have a range of content, as well features that try to build community, such as chat rooms, forums, and contests, but without these two messages a commerce site will be hard put to accomplish any commerce.

The e-commerce Trust Study from Studio Archetype/Sapient and Cheskin Research presents some interesting analysis on "the nature of those elements that communicate 'trust' in e-commerce sites, be they transactional or graphical". According to this study:

The factors that produce a sense of trustworthiness need to be identified, in their entirety. Their interactions need to be understood, and their relative importance determined. Understanding the roles of these different factors would allow online retailers to ease consumers' concerns, and could hasten the maturation of Web retailing.

The report describes 6 main components (along with a total of 28 sub-components which I won't mention here) of a commerce site that suggest trustworthiness.

(1) Seals of Approval

Symbols, like VeriSign and Visa, designed to re-assure the visitor that security has been established. The companies that provide these seals of approval are referred to in this report as security brands.

(2) Brand

The corporation's promise to deliver specific attributes and its credibility based on reputation and the visitor's possible previous experience.

(3) Navigation

The ease of finding what the visitor seeks.

(4) Fulfillment

Clearly indicates how orders will be processed, and provides information on how to seek recourse if there are problems.

(5) Presentation

Design attributes that connote quality and professionalism.

(6) Technology

State of the art connotes professionalism, even if it's difficult to use.

This study has some valuable insights into user attitudes towards trust and e-commerce sites, and is clearly required reading for anyone interested in understanding online commerce. I do, however, have some issues with the report.

First, this analysis seems to consider online commerce in isolation. E-commerce is a new kind of shopping experience in a new medium, but this experience is still new enough that the vast majority of people who buy online learned how to buy offline. Addressing e-commerce in isolation presumes that it can be studied as its own phenomenon with no experiential antecedents, which is unrealistic and will likely produce misunderstandings of e-commerce and user behavior.

If this study relies on an assumption that e-commerce is simply a modal variation of traditional commerce, then any analysis will be flawed. The fact is that the customer's experience of the characteristics of traditional commerce does not map to online commerce, forcing the customer to seek imperfect analogs. The e-commerce Trust Study would be more accurate if it had addressed the chasm between what customers understand from traditional commerce, and what online commerce can possibly address.

Second, I think this report is a bit free in its lack of clear differentiation between what the merchant cando—suggest that it is trustworthy—and what the user mustdo—decide whether or not to trust the merchant. Granted, there is no checklist for commerce design that specifies everything that must be done a certain way to be correct, and no checklist that has a test for everything that might be done incorrectly. Commerce site designers, however, must understand that they cannot code trust into a site, they can only suggest trust. Trust is a property controlled by the customer.

4. Using Design to Communicate With the User

The obvious method to convince users to buy from your commerce site is to provide the customer with a pleasant experience. Reduce the chances of negative events, or the misapprehension of events as negative. Keep in mind that the user will move around your site and read your text, and ultimately decide on whether to buy from you based on judgments of their experience with your site; you don't know what will make them say no, so you can't afford to be haphazard with your message cues.

Some trouble points that deserve attention.

(1) Make Your Site Look Professional

You don't have to spend huge amounts of money to hire a bleeding edge design house, just make sure your site doesn't look amateurish. Choose your fonts, color schemes and graphic cues carefully.

(2) Polish Your Information Architecture

Organize your information so it makes sense to customers who may not live and breath your product. You should not be required to be an expert in your product in order to navigate your catalog, and you should have multiple logical tracks to accessing any product.

(3) Polish Your Navigation

Don't force your customers to dig to find what they want to buy, and then dig to find out how to buy it.

(4) Answer Questions Pro-actively

Research the potential problems customers may have using your site and document them. Design your FAQs carefully. Include help text in your commerce flow. Every time a customer must communicate with your customer service or webmaster teams, you risk annoying the customer. The "correct" approach to customer communications is that every email is an "opportunity", but most online commerce sites don't have the staff to convert complaints into happy solutions.

(5) Refine Your Commerce Track

Anticipate the needs and behaviors of your typical customer—if necessary creating user profiles—and design your commerce track (which Peter Merholtz describes as the "commerce tunnel") to accommodate those users. Most users have an expectation of what makes up the process of purchasing, so if your site throws up what seem to be arbitrary, intrusive or threatening barriers to purchasing you will lose customers and sales.

(6) Address Privacy Concerns Explicitly

Privacy and the ownership of personal information is a big issue. Don't be vague or wishy-washy where the customer's personal information is concerned. If you require the user to give address or e-mail information, explain how you will use it. If you will use e-mail info to send the user non-order related notices, provide an opt-out mechanism.

(7) Set Expectations Carefully

Explain the steps to completing a purchase, and explain the factors that will affect shipment, timing, returns, crediting, etc. Set expectations of service that your site can meet. Aim to under-promise and over-deliver.

Part 3   Academic Reading   学术阅读

Passage   SWOT Analysis SWOT 分析法

1. What's SWOT Analysis

SWOT analysis (Strengths, Weaknesses, Opportunities and Threats) is a tool for auditing an organization and its environment. It is the first stage of planning and helps marketers to focus on key issues. SWOT stands for strengths, weaknesses, opportunities, and threats. Strengths and weaknesses are internal factors. Opportunities and threats are external factors.

In SWOT, strengths and weaknesses are internal factors. For example: a strength could be your specialist marketing expertise, a new innovative product or service, location of your business, quality processes and procedures and any other aspect of your business that adds value to your product or service; A weakness could be lack of marketing expertise, undifferentiated products or services (i.e. in relation to your competitors), location of your business, poor quality goods or services and damaged reputation.

Opportunities and threats are external factors. For example: an opportunity could be a developing market such as the internet, mergers, joint ventures or strategic alliances, moving into new market segments that offer improved profits, a new international market, a market vacated by an ineffective competitor; A threat could be a new competitor in your home market, price wars with competitors, a competitor who has a new, innovative product or service, competitors who have superior access to channels of distribution, taxation is introduced on your product or service.

There are some simple rules for successful SWOT analysis. ①Be realistic about the strengths and weaknesses of your organization when conducting SWOT analysis. ②SWOT analysis should distinguish between where your organization is today, and where it could be in the future. SWOT should always be specific. Avoid grey areas. ③Always apply SWOT in relation to your competition, i.e. better than or worse than your competition. ④Keep your SWOT short and simple. Avoid complexity and over analysis. ⑤SWOT is subjective.

Once key issues have been identified with your SWOT analysis, they feed into marketing objectives. SWOT can be used in conjunction with other tools for audit and analysis, such as **PEST analysis** and Porter's **Five-Forces analysis**. So SWOT is a very popular tool with marketing students because it is quick and easy to learn. During the SWOT exercise, list factors in the relevant boxes. It's that simple. Below are some FREE examples of SWOT analysis—click to go straight to them.

(1) PEST Analysis

It is very important that an organization considers its environment before beginning the marketing process. In fact, environmental analysis should be continuous and feed all aspects of planning. The organization's marketing environment is made up of:

① The internal environment, e.g. staff (or internal customers), office technology, wages and finance, etc.

② The micro-environment, e.g. our external customers, agents and distributors, suppliers, our competitors, etc.

③ The macro-environment, e.g. Political (and legal) forces, Economic forces, Sociocultural forces, and Technological forces. These are known as PEST factors.

The political arena has a huge influence upon the regulation of businesses, and the spending power of consumers and other businesses. You must consider issues such as:

① How stable is the political environment?

Unit 5
International Marketing and Management 国际营销与管理

② Will government policy influence laws that regulate or tax your business?
③ What is the government's position on marketing ethics?
④ What is the government's policy on the economy?
⑤ Does the government have a view on culture and religion?
⑥ Is the government involved in trading agreements such as EU, NAFTA, ASEAN, or others?

Marketers need to consider the state of a trading economy in the short and long-terms. This is especially true when planning for international marketing. You need to look at:
① Interest rates.
② The level of inflation Employment level per capita.
③ Long-term prospects for the economy Gross Domestic Product (GDP) per capita, and so on.

The social and cultural influences on business vary from country to country. It is very important that such factors are considered. Factors include:
① What is the dominant religion?
② What are attitudes to foreign products and services?
③ Does language impact upon the diffusion of products onto markets?
④ How much time do consumers have for leisure?
⑤ What are the roles of men and women within society?
⑥ How long are the population living? Are the older generations wealthy?
⑦ Do the population have a strong/weak opinion on green issues?

Technology is vital for competitive advantage, and is a major driver of globalization. Consider the following points.
① Does technology allow for products and services to be made more cheaply and to a better standard of quality?
② Do the technologies offer consumers and businesses more innovative products and services such as Internet banking, new generation mobile telephones, etc?
③ How is distribution changed by new technologies, e.g. books via the Internet, flight tickets, auctions, etc?
④ Does technology offer companies a new way to communicate with consumers, e.g. banners, Customer Relationship Management (CRM), etc?

(2) Five Forces Analysis

Five Forces Analysis helps the marketer to contrast a competitive environment. It has similarities with other tools for environmental audit, such as PEST analysis, but tends to focus on the single, stand alone, business or SBU (Strategic Business Unit) rather than a single product or range of products. For example, Dell would analyze the market for Business Computers, i.e. one of its SBUs. Five forces analysis looks at five key areas namely the threat of entry, the power of buyers, the power of suppliers, the threat of substitutes, and competitive rivalry.

① The threat of entry.

a. Economies of scale, e.g. the benefits associated with bulk purchasing.

b. The high or low cost of entry, e.g. how much will it cost for the latest technology?

c. Ease of access to distribution channels, e.g. do our competitors have the distribution channels sewn up?

d. Cost advantages not related to the size of the company, e.g. personal contacts or knowledge that larger companies do not own or learning curve effects.

e. Will competitors retaliate?

f. Government action, e.g. will new laws be introduced that will weaken our competitive position?

g. How important is differentiation? e.g. The Champagne brand cannot be copied. This desensitizes the influence of the environment.

h. This is high where there a few, large players in a market, e.g. the large grocery chains.

i. If there are a large number of undifferentiated, small suppliers, e.g. small farming businesses supplying the large grocery chains.

j. The cost of switching between suppliers is low, e.g. from one fleet supplier of trucks to another.

② The power of suppliers.

The power of suppliers tends to be a reversal of the power of buyers.

a. Where the switching costs are high, e.g. switching from one software supplier to another.

b. Power is high where the brand is powerful, e.g. Cadillac, Pizza Hut, Microsoft.

c. There is a possibility of the supplier integrating forward, e.g. brewers buying bars.

d. Customers are fragmented (not in clusters) so that they have little bargaining power, e.g. gas/petrol stations in remote places.

③ The threat of substitutes.

a. Where there is product-for-product substitution, e.g. e-mail for fax.

b. Where there is substitution of need, e.g. better toothpaste reduces the need for dentists.

c. Where there is generic substitution (competing for the currency in your pocket), e.g. video suppliers compete with travel companies.

d. We could always do without, e.g. cigarettes.

④ Competitive rivalry.

This is most likely to be high where entry is likely; there is the threat of substitute products, and suppliers and buyers in the market attempt to control. This is why it is always seen in the center of the diagram.

2. Examples of SWOT Analysis

(1) SWOT Analysis Apple

① Strengths.

a. Apple is a very successful company. Sales of its iPod music player had increased its second quarter profits to $320 (June 2005). The favorable brand perception had also increased sales of Macintosh computers. So iPod gives the company access to a whole new series of segments that buy into other parts of the Apple brand. Sale of its notebooks products is also very strong, and represents a huge contribution to income for Apple.

b. Brand is all-important. Apple is one of the most established and healthy IT brands in the World, and has a very loyal set of enthusiastic customers that advocate the brand. Such a powerful loyalty means that Ample not only recruits new customers, it retains them, i.e. they come back for more products and services from Apple, and the company also has the opportunity to extend new products to them, for example the iPod.

② Weaknesses.

a. It is reported that the Apple iPod Nano may have a faulty screen. The company has commented that a batch of its product has screens that break under impact, and the company is replacing all faulty items. This is in addition to problems with early iPods that had faulty batteries, whereby the company offered customers free battery cases.

b. There is pressure on Apple to increase the price of its music download file, from the music industry itself. Many of these companies make more money from iTunes (i.e. downloadable music files) than from their original CD sales. Apple has sold about 22 million iPod digital music players and more than 500 million songs though its iTunes music store. It accounts for 82% of all legally downloaded music in the U.S. The company is resolute, but if it gives in to the music producers, it may be perceived as a commercial weakness.

c. Early in 2005 Apple announced that it was to end its long-standing relationship with IBM as a chip supplier, and that it was about to switch to Intel. Some industry specialists commented that the swap could confuse Apple's consumers.

③ Opportunities.

a. Apple has the opportunity to develop its iTunes and music player technology into a mobile phone format. The Rokr mobile phone device was developed by Motorola. It has a colour screen, stereo speakers and an advance camera system. A version of Apple's iTunes music store has been developed for the phone so users can manage the tracks they store on it. Downloads are available via a USB cable, and software on the handset pauses music if a phone call comes in. New technologies and strategic alliances offer opportunities for Apple.

b. Podcasts are downloadable radio shows that can be downloaded from the Internet, and then played back on iPods and other MP3 devices at the convenience of the listener. The listener can subscribe to Podcasts for free, and ultimately revenue could be generated from paid for subscription or through revenue generated from sales of other downloads.

④ Threats.

a. The biggest threat to IT companies such as Apple is the very high level of competition in the technology markets. Being successful attracts competition, and Apple works very hard on research and development and marketing in order to retain its competitive position. The popularity of iPod and Apple Mac are subject to demand, and will be affected if economies begin to falter and demand falls for their products.

b. There is also a high product substitution effect in the innovative and fast moving IT consumables market. So iPod and MP3 rule today, but only yesterday it was CD, DAT, and Vinyl. Tomorrow's technology might be completely different. Wireless technologies could replace the need for a physical music player.

c. In 2005 Apple won a legal case that forced Bloggers to name the sources of information that pre-empted the launch of new Apple products. It was suspect that Apple's own employees had leaked confidential information about their new Asteroid product. The three individuals prosecuted, all owned Apple tribute sites, and were big fans of the company's products. The blogs had appeared on their sites, and they were forced to reveal their source. The ruling saw commercial confidentiality as more important as the right to speech of individuals. Apple are vulnerable to leaks that could cost them profits.

(2) SWOT Analysis China Mobile

① Corporate overview.

China Mobile Limited was started in 1997. Originally it was called China Telecom (Hong Kong) and then China Mobile (Hong Kong) and finally China Mobile Limited as we know it today. Its public offering in 1997 generated capital of USD $2.5 million, and a further massive investment of global capital (around USD $600 million) was made in 2004.

Today it trades in 31 provinces of China and essentially offers a Global System for Mobile Communications (GSM) which covers almost the entire nation. The business makes money from its voice-based services and other value-added services such as SMS text, mobile e-mail and similar services.

International Marketing and Management 国际营销与管理   Unit 5

② Strengths.

a. China Mobile was listed fifth in Millward Brown's Brandz Top 100 Brands in 2007. This would have be unheard of 10 years ago (or even less). The news means that the company is becoming more than a business since it is now also a brand, i.e. possessing brand equity and brand value. Other Chinese brands to break the top 100 were the Bank of China, the Chinese Construction Bank and IBBC. It is argued by many that Chinese companies are not strong in relation to marketing but perhaps things are changing.

b. The company has made good profits over recent years.

c. China Mobile has gone down the acquisition trail on a number of occasions. In its early days it took over Jiangsu Mobile (1997). Other important acquisitions include Fujian Mobile, Henan Mobile, and Hainan Mobile (1999); and Beijing Mobile, Shanghai Mobile, Tianjin Mobile and Hebei Mobile (2000). These developments have delivered strong growth.

d. China Mobile is number one in the Chinese market. It recorded a 67.5% market share in 2006. It is the world's largest digital mobile company, and serves more customers than any other mobile supplier.

③ Weaknesses.

a. According to the head of China Mobile, China's home-grown mobile technology is a few years behind that of its international competitors since it was having problems with handsets. Essentially 3G technology was lagging behind. Part of the problem was the choice to swap to TD-SCDMA's network which many would consider inferior to the 3G technology offered by European and American alternatives (which their competitors have decided to adopt).

b. The company is not globally diversified. Telecoms companies tend to trade in more than one country, usually through acquisition, joint-ventures or strategic alliances (for example see the SWOT analysis of BhartiAirtel). This may leave the company exposed if the Chinese market were to go into a deep or sustained decline.

④ Opportunities.

a. The Chinese economy has undergone enormous growth, which has lead to the huge demand for mobile telephones, devices and technologies. According to the Chinese Government, China is the world's largest mobile market with 520 million mobile phone users. This number could reach 600 million by 2010.

b. Budget users in China are driving growth in the mobile telecoms sector. China Mobile reported a net profit between January and March 2008 of around 24.1bn yuan ($3.4bn; $2.2bn) which is a rise of 37% on 2007 according to BBC News.

c. Since the cities have become saturated, much of the new growth is predicted for rural

China and it is this segment that is most likely to be targeted by the large operators. 3G technologies provide the largest opportunity for China Telecom.

⑤ Threats.

a. New subscribers are mainly low-use, low-value. So average revenue is falling as the mobile phone market matures and the market becomes more price competitive. So mobile phone suppliers are awaiting the introduction of 3G mobile technologies to rejuvenate the market and stimulate demand as Chinese customers consume the new added value services.

b. China Mobile could face more competition in the future as the Chinese Government plans to allow more operators into the market. China Mobile has 70% of the 2G market in China. China Unicom wants to become the biggest 3G operator, and China Telecom aims to win 15% of the 3G market by 2010.

c. China Mobile has a number of service obligations under agreements with the Chinese (PRC) Government. So the business may be obliged to provide unprofitable services that pay a social dividend. Added to this the Ministry of Information and Industry has allocated a limited frequency (44MHz) to the company which will not support large numbers of subscribers in the future.

(3) SWOT Analysis Nike, Inc.

① Strengths.

a. Nike is a very competitive organization. Phil Knight (Founder and CEO) is often quoted as saying that "Business is war without bullets". Nike has a healthy dislike of is competitors. At the Atlanta Olympics, Reebok went to the expense of sponsoring the games. Nike did not. However Nike sponsored the top athletes and gained valuable coverage.

b. Nike has no factories. It does not tie up cash in buildings and manufacturing workers. This makes a very lean organization. Nike is strong at research and development, as is evidenced by its evolving and innovative product range. They then manufacture wherever they can produce high quality product at the lowest possible price. If prices rise, and products can be made more cheaply elsewhere (to the same or better specification), Nike will move production.

c. Nike is a global brand. It is the number one sports brand in the World. Its famous "Swoosh" is instantly recognisable, and Phil Knight even has it tattooed on his ankle.

② Weaknesses.

a. The organization does have a diversified range of sports products. However, the income of the business is still heavily dependent upon its share of the footwear market. This may leave it vulnerable if for any reason its market share erodes.

b. The retail sector is very price sensitive. Nike does have its own retailer in Nike Town. However, most of its income is derived from selling into retailers. Retailers tend to offer a very similar experience to the consumer. Can you tell one sports retailer from another? So margins tend to get squeezed as retailers try to pass some of the low price competition pressure onto Nike.

③ Opportunities.

a. Product development offers Nike many opportunities. The brand is fiercely defended by its owners whom truly believe that Nike is not a fashion brand. However, like it or not, consumers that wear Nike product do not always buy it to participate in sport. Some would argue that in youth culture especially, Nike is a fashion brand. This creates its own opportunities, since product could become unfashionable before it wears out, i.e. consumers need to replace shoes.

b. There is also the opportunity to develop products such as sport wear, sunglasses and jewellery. Such high value items do tend to have associated with them, high profits.

c. The business could also be developed internationally, building upon its strong global brand recognition. There are many markets that have the disposable income to spend on high value sports goods. For example, emerging markets such as China and India have a new richer generation of consumers. There are also global marketing events that can be utilized to support the brand such as the World Cup (soccer) and The Olympics.

④ Threats.

a. Nike is exposed to the international nature of trade. It buys and sells in different currencies and so costs and margins are not stable over long periods of time. Such an exposure could mean that Nike may be manufacturing and/or selling at a loss. This is an issue that faces all global brands.

b. The market for sports shoes and garments is very competitive. The model developed by Phil Knight in his Stamford Business School days (high value branded product manufactured at a low cost) is now commonly used and to an extent is no longer a basis for sustainable competitive advantage. Competitors are developing alternative brands to take away Nike's market share.

c. As discussed above in weaknesses, the retail sector is becoming price competitive. This ultimately means that consumers are shopping around for a better deal. So if one store charges a price for a pair of sports shoes, the consumer could go to the store along the street to compare prices for the exactly the same item, and buy the cheaper of the two. Such consumer price sensitivity is a potential external threat to Nike.

(4) SWOT Analysis McDonald's

① Strengths.

a. McDonald's has been a thriving business since 1955 and 20 of the top 50 corporate staff employees started as a restaurant level employee. In addition, 67,000 McDonald's restaurant managers and assistant managers were promoted from restaurant staff. Fortune Magazine 2005 listed McDonald's as the "Best Place to Work for Minorities". McDonald's invests more than $1 billion annually in training its staff, and every year more than 250,000 employees graduate from McDonald's training facility, Hamburger University.

b. The business is ranked number one in Fortune Magazine's 2008 list of most admired food service companies.

c. One of the world's most recognizable logos (the Golden Arches) and spokes character (Ronald McDonald the clown). According to the Packard Children's Hospital's Center for Healthy Weight children age 3 to 5 were given food in the McDonald's packaging and then given the same food without the packaging, and they preferred the food in the McDonald's packaging every single time.

d. McDonald's is a community oriented, socially responsible company. They run Ronald McDonald House facilities, which provide room and board, food and sibling support at a cost of only $10 a day for families with children needing extensive hospital care. Ronald McDonald Houses are located in more than 259 local communities worldwide, and Ronald McDonald Care Mobile programs offers cost effective medical, dental and education services to children. They also sponsor Olympic athletes.

e. They are a global company operating more than 23,500 restaurants in 109 countries. By being spread out in different regions, this gives them the ability to weather economic fluctuations which are localized by country. They can also operate effectively in an economic downturn due to the social need to seek out comfort foods.

f. They successfully and easily adapt their global restaurants to appeal to the cultural differences. For example, they serve lamb burgers in India and in the Middle East, they provide separate entrances for families and single women.

g. Approximately 85% of McDonald's restaurant businesses world-wide are owned and operated by franchisees. All franchisees are independent, full-time operators and McDonald's was named Entrepreneur's number-one franchise in 1997. They have global locations in all major airports, and cities, along the highways, tourist locations, theme parks and inside Wal-Mart.

h. They have an efficient, assembly line style of food preparation. In addition they have a systemization and duplication of all their food prep processes in every restaurant.

i. McDonald's uses only 100% pure USDA inspected beef, no fillers or additives. Additionally the produce is farm fresh. McDonald's serves 100% farm raised chicken no fillers or additives and only grade-A eggs. McDonald's foods are purchased from only certified and inspected suppliers. McDonald's works closely with ranchers, growers and suppliers to ensure food quality and freshness.

Unit 5
International Marketing and Management 国际营销与管理

j. McDonald's only serves name brand processed items such as Dannon Yogurt, Kraft Cheese, Nestle Chocolate, Dasani Water, Newman's Own Salad Dressings, Heinz Ketchup, Minute Maid Juice.

k. McDonald's takes food safety very seriously. More than 2,000 inspections checks are performed at every stage of the food process. McDonald's are required to run through 72 safety protocols every day to ensure the food is maintained in a clean contaminate free environment.

l. McDonald's was the first restaurant of its type to provide consumers with nutrition information. Nutrition information is printed on all packaging and more recently added to the McDonald's Internet site. McDonald's offers salads, fruit, roasted chicken, bottled water and other low fat and calorie conscious alternatives.

② Weaknesses.

a. Their test marketing for pizza failed to yield a substantial product. Leaving them much less able to compete with fast food pizza chains.

b. High employee turnover in their restaurants leads to more money being spent on training.

c. They have yet to capitalize on the trend towards organic foods.

d. McDonald's have problems with fluctuations in operating and net profits which ultimately impact investor relations. Operating profit was $3,984 million (2005) $4,433 million (2006) and $3,879 million (2007). Net profits were $2,602 million (2005), $3,544 million (2006) and $2,395 million (2007).

③ Opportunities.

a. In today's health conscious societies the introduction of a healthy hamburger is a great opportunity. They would be the first QSR (Quick Service Restaurant) to have FDA approval on marketing a low fat low calorie hamburger with low calorie combo alternatives. Currently McDonald's and its competition health choice items do not include hamburgers.

b. They have industrial, Formica restaurant settings; they could provide more upscale restaurant settings, like the one they have in New York City on Broadway, to appeal to a more upscale target market.

c. Provide optional allergen free food items, such as gluten free and peanut free.

d. In 2008 the business directed efforts at the breakfast, chicken, beverage and convenience categories. For example, hot specialist coffees not only secure sales, but also mean that restaurants get increasing numbers of customer visits. In 2009 McDonald's saw the full benefits of a venture into beverages.

④ Threats.

a. They are a benchmark for creating "cradle to grave" marketing. They entice children as young as one year old into their restaurants with special meals, toys, playgrounds and popular movie character tie-ins. Children grow up eating and enjoying McDonald's and then continue into adulthood. They have been criticized by many parent advocate groups for their marketing practices towards children which are seen as marginally ethical.

b. They have been sued multiple times for having "unhealthy" food, allegedly with addictive additives, contributing to the obesity epidemic in America. In 2004, Michael Spulock filmed the documentary Super Size Me, where he went on an all McDonald's diet for 30 days and wound up getting cirrhosis of the liver. This documentary was a direct attack on the QSR industry as a whole and blamed them for America's obesity epidemic. Due in part to the documentary, McDonald's no longer pushes the super size option at the dive thru window.

c. Any contamination of the food supply, especially e-coli.

d. Major competitors, like Burger King, Starbucks, Taco Bell, Wendy's, KFC and any mid-range sit-down restaurants.

(5) SWOT Analysis Time Warner

① Strengths.

a. Dominant market share.

Time Warner is not only a dominant U.S. company, it is one of the world's largest media companies. Its pre-eminence in the U.S. market is evident in the publication of 23 magazines, such as, Sports Illustrated, Time, InStyle, Real Simple, People, Fortune and Southern Living. The company also boasts nearly 50 websites internationally, such as People.com, SI.com and CNN Money.com.

Publishers Information Bureau rates Time Warner the largest magazine publisher in the U.S. based upon advertising revenues received, while Nielsen Media Research and Media Metrix state that the company's websites average over 29 million unique visitors monthly.

Time Warner's AOL Web Content Services Division reached 75 million unique visitors in 2009 according to comScore Media Metrix data. AOL's internet access subscription service is one of the largest in the U.S. and MapQuest is one of the most prominent map and direction service in the U.S.

Consider also, Time Warner's dominance of television programming. It distributes programming in more than 200 countries through its Warner Bros Television Group (WBTVG). In the U.S., Turner's entertainment networks include TBS, with more than 90 million U.S. households as in 2008; and TNT, with over 90 million households in the U.S.

Its presence even reaches into the contemporary cartoon genre such as the Cartoon Network (including Adult Swim, an overnight block of contemporary animation airing in 2008, which boasted approximately 97.7 million households in the U.S.

Time Warner is also prominent in the classic movie and cable television news areas. Its television news services, reached over 95 million U.S. television households in 2008. Meanwhile, CNN operated 46 news bureaus and editorial operations, including 13 located in the U.S. In addition, Time Warner's HBO is a pay television service (including its sister service, Cinemax), which collectively had approximately 40.9 million subscriptions as of FY2008.

b. Substantial entertainment programming.

Time Warner produces and distributes theatrical motion pictures, television shows, animation and other programming such as videogames. In addition, the company distributes DVDs containing filmed entertainment produced or acquired by the company's various content-producing subsidiaries and divisions, including Warner Bros. Pictures, Warner Bros. Television, New Line, Home Box Office and Turner Broadcasting System. LEGO Batman, Speed Racer and Guinness World Records, and co-published Lego Indiana Jones are among the interactive videogames produced by Time Warner through its subsidiaries.

② Weaknesses.

Substantial Dependence on the U.S. markets although, the company has operations across South America, Europe, Asia Pacific and Middle East, the U.S. is its primary market. Over 80% of its total revenues come from the U.S. The slumping U.S. economy may negatively impact demand for the Time Warner 's products and services.

Recent data show a downward trend in revenues for Time-Warner's AOL division. In FY 2008 AOL reported a drop in revenues from $4,165 in 2006 to $7, 786 million in FY 2008, representing a negative compounded annual growth rate (CAGR) of 27%. The decline is primarily due to the decrease in the number of domestic AOL brand subscribers and the sale of AOL's German access business. Also, AOL revenues as a percentage of total revenues declined 17.8% during the same period. The declining performance of AOL may negatively impact the company's overall revenue and profitability.

③ Opportunities.

The company has formed alliances with several leading companies in the media and entertainment industry. In October 2009, Warner Home Video (WHV) entered into a multi-year alliance with Sesame Workshop, a nonprofit educational organization. Under the terms of the agreement, WHV will exclusively distribute multiple Sesame Street titles, including the Sesame Street library.

In August 2009, Time-Warner and The Nielsen Company signed an agreement to provides Nielsen services to Time Warner's broadcast, cable, syndication business units and affiliates, including Turner Broadcasting, The CW Television Network, HBO, Warner Brothers Domestic TV Distribution, Time Inc., RET Media and station WPCH. In addition, Time Warner and YouTube signed an online video distribution agreement, which allows Warner Bros. Entertainment and Turner Broadcasting System to program videos on YouTube using a Time Warner embeddable player.

MBC Group and Warner Bros. International Television Distribution (WBITD) signed a multiyear programming deal in April 2009. These are just some of the multiple partnerships which will enable the company to extend its reach and increase its subscriber base in the coming years.

④ Threats.

a. Competitive environment.

Time Warner has formidable competition in each of its major business segments. The company's AOL Division must face off against such firms as Google, Yahoo and Microsoft. In addition, MySpace, Facebook and Fox Interactive Media also compete with AOL for internet based revenues. Also, other traditional media firms have begun to offer their own internet services, among them are WPP Group (24/7 Real Media) and ValueClick. Broadband access providers also compete against AOL for internet subscribers.

Increasingly, Time Warner's film entertainment business faces intense competition from new market entrees such as websites with internet streaming, user-generated content and interactive games. Alternative distribution systems such as cable and satellite provide competition for Turner Networks and Turner's websites. With so many competitors in the industry there may be a scarcity of producers, directors, writers, actors and other skilled areas.

In recent years, competitors have launched new magazines and websites in the celebrity, women's service and business sectors, these ventures compete directly with Time Warners's People, InStyle, Real Simple, and Fortune magazines. Such intense competition as described above, could impact Time Warner pricing decisions and in turn effect revenues and market share.

b. Unauthorized distribution of content.

Time Warner is increasingly impacted by the piracy of its television, motion pictures programming, DVD, and video games. Piracy is on the rise due to technological advances which allow thieves to create, transmit and distribute high quality unauthorized copies of content. This unauthorized distribution has the potential to reduce Time Warner's revenues. Time Warner is also vulnerable to content theft in countries where it operates if those countries have weak laws protecting intellectual property or enforcement is lax.

c. Dependence on Google.

Google is the main web search provider for nearly all of Time Warner's AOL network and products. AOL has agreed to use Google's algorithmic search and sponsored links on an exclusive basis through December 19, 2010. Failure to renew the agreement with Google will adversely affect the company's operations. In addition any unilateral change Google may make in pricing, algorithms or advertising terms, could have a significant negative impact.

Part 4   Reading Comprehension   阅读理解

Passage 1   The Intuition of Senior Management 高级管理者的直觉

The majority of successful senior managers do not closely follow the classical rational model of first clarifying goals, assessing the problem, formulating options, estimating likelihoods of success, making a decision, and only then taking action to implement the decision. Rather, in their day-by-day tactical maneuvers, these senior executives rely on what is vaguely termed intuition to manage a network of interrelated problems that require them to deal with ambiguity, inconsistency, novelty, and surprise, and to integrate action into the process of thinking.

Generations of writers on management have recognized that some practicing managers rely heavily on intuition. In general, however, such writers display a poor grasp of what intuition is. Some see it as the opposite of rationality; others view it as an excuse for capriciousness.

Isenberg's recent research on the cognitive processes of senior managers reveals that managers' intuition is neither of these. Rather, senior managers use intuition in at least five distinct ways. First, they intuitively sense when a problem exists. Second, managers rely on intuition to perform well-learned behavior patterns rapidly. This intuition is not arbitrary or irrational, but is based on years of painstaking practice and hands-on experience that build skills. A third function of intuition is to synthesize isolated bits of data and practice into an integrated picture, often in an Aha! Experience. Fourth, some managers use intuition as a check on the results of more rational analysis. Most senior executives are familiar with the formal decision analysis models and tools, and those who use such systematic methods for reaching decisions are occasionally leery of solutions suggested by these methods which run counter to their sense of the correct course of action. Finally, managers can use intuition to bypass in-depth analysis and move rapidly to engender a plausible solution. Used in this way, intuition is an almost instantaneous cognitive process in which a manager recognizes familiar patterns.

One of the implications of the intuitive style of executive management is that thinking is inseparable from acting. Since managers often know what is right before they can analyze and explain it, they frequently act first and explain later. Analysis is inextricably tied to action in thinking/acting cycles, in which managers develop thoughts about their companies and organizations not by analyzing a problematic situation and then acting, but by acting and analyzing in close concert.

Given the great uncertainty of many of the management issues that they face, senior managers often instigate a course of action simply to learn more about an issue. They then use the results of the action to develop a more complete understanding of the issue. One implication of thinking/acting cycles is that action is often part of defining the problem, not just of implementing the solution.

1. According to the text, senior managers use intuition in all of the following ways EXCEPT to (   ).

   [A] speed up of the creation of a solution to a problem

   [B] identify a problem

   [C] bring together disparate facts

   [D] stipulate clear goals

2. The text suggests which of the following about the writers on management mentioned in line 1, paragraph 2? (   )

   [A] They have criticized managers for not following the classical rational model of decision analysis

   [B] They have not based their analyses on a sufficiently large sample of actual managers

   [C] They have relied in drawing their conclusions on what managers say rather than on what managers do

   [D] They have misunderstood how managers use intuition in making business decisions

3. It can be inferred from the text that which of the following would most probably be one major difference in behavior between Manager X, who uses intuition to reach decisions, and Manager Y, who uses only formal decision analysis? (   )

   [A] Manager X analyzes first and then acts; Manager Y does not

   [B] Manager X checks possible solutions to a problem by systematic analysis; Manager Y does not

   [C] Manager X takes action in order to arrive at the solution to a problem; Manager Y does not

   [D] Manager Y draws on years of hands-on experience in creating a solution to a problem; Manager X does not

4. The text provides support for which of the following statements? (   )

   [A] Managers who rely on intuition are more successful than those who rely on formal decision analysis

Unit 5
International Marketing and Management 国际营销与管理

[B] Managers cannot justify their intuitive decisions

[C] Managers' intuition works contrary to their rational and analytical skills

[D] Intuition enables managers to employ their practical experience more efficiently

5. Which of the following best describes the organization of the first paragraph of the text? (　　)

[A] An assertion is made and a specific supporting example is given

[B] A conventional model is dismissed and an alternative introduced

[C] The results of recent research are introduced and summarized

[D] Two opposing points of view are presented and evaluated

Passage 2　Advertisement 广告

Foods are overwhelmingly the most advertised group of all consumer products in the United States. Food products lead in expenditures for network and spot television advertisements, discount coupons, trading stamps, contests, and other forms of premium advertising. In other media—newspapers, magazines, newspaper supplements, billboards, and radio—food advertising expenditures rank near the top. Food manufacturers spend more on advertising than any other manufacturing group, and the nation's grocery stores rank first among all retailers. Through the 1970's, highly processed foods have accounted for the bulk of total advertising.

Almost all coupons, electronic advertising, national printed media advertising, consumer premiums (other than trading stamps) as well as most push promotion come from processed and packaged food products. In 1978, breakfast cereals, soft drinks, candy and other desserts, oils and salad dressings, coffee, and prepared foods accounted for only an estimated 20 percent of the consumer food dollar. Yet these items accounted for about one half of all media advertising.

By contrast, highly perishable foods such as unprocessed meats, poultry, fish and eggs, fruits and vegetables, and dairy products accounted for over half of the consumer food-at-home dollar. Yet these products accounted for less than 8 percent of national media advertising in 1978, and virtually no discount coupons. These products tend to be most heavily advertised by the retail sector in local newspaper, where they account for an estimated 40 percent of retail grocery newspaper ads.

When measured against total food-at-home expenditures, total measured food advertising accounts for between 3 and 3.7 cents out of every dollar spent on food in the nation's grocery stores. A little less than one cent of these amounts is accounted for by electronic advertising (mostly television) while incentives account for 0.6 cents. The printed media accounts for 0.5 cents and about one-third of one cent is comprised of discount coupon redemptions. The estimate for the cost of push promotion ranged from 0.7 to 1.4 cents. This range is necessary because of the difficulty in separating non-promotional aspects of direct selling-transportation, technical, and other related services.

Against this gross consumer must be weighed the joint products or services provided by advertising. In the case of electronic advertising, the consumer who views commercial television receives entertainment, while readers of magazines and newspapers receive reduced prices on these publications. The consumer pays directly for some premiums, but also receives nonfood merchandise as an incentive to purchase the product. The "benefits" must, therefore, be subtracted from the gross cost to the consumer to fully assess the net cost of advertising.

Also significant are the impacts of advertising on food demand, nutrition, and competition among food manufactures. The bulk of manufacturers' advertising is concentrated on a small portion of consumer food products. Has advertising changed the consumption of these highly processed products relative to more perishable foods such as meats, produce, and dairy products? Has the nutritional content of the U.S. food consumption been influenced by food advertisings? Has competition among manufacturers and retailers been enhance or weakened by advertising? These are important questions and warrant continued research.

1. The author's attitude toward advertising can be characterized as (   ).

   [A] admiring   [B] condemning   [C] uncertain   [D] inquisitive

2. The term "push promotion" means (   ).

   [A] coupon redemption   [B] retail advertising
   [C] direct selling   [D] advertising in trade journals

3. The author implies that advertising costs (   ).

   [A] should be discounted by the benefits of advertising to the consumer
   [B] are greater for restaurants than for at home foods
   [C] are much higher in the United Stated than any where else in the world
   [D] cause highly processed foods to outsell unprocessed outsell foods

4. The purpose of the article is to (   ).

   [A] warm about rising food advertising costs
   [B] describe the costs of food advertising and the issues yet to be understood about its effects
   [C] congratulate the food industry on its effective advertising
   [D] calculate the final balance sheet for food advertising

5. According to the passage, all of the following are definitely false EXCEPT (   ).

[A] more food is advertised in newspapers than on television

[B] less money is spent advertising food than automobiles

[C] more of the food advertising budget is probably spent on push promotion than on television ads

[D] less money is spent on food store advertising than on clothing store ads

Part 5　课 文 注 释

1. The replication of a company's business system in various locations around the world does not, however, represent a long-term formula for profitable growth and, ultimately, international companies face the need to optimize their business globally by adopting a global mode of operation.

翻译：然而把一个公司的业务系统在世界各地重复并不是可取得盈利增长的长期方案，最终，国际公司便面临这样一种局面，需要通过采取全球性的经营方式，在全球范围内有效地发展其业务。

2. To successfully compete globally, rather than simply operate domestically, companies should emphasize:①global configuration of marketing activities; ②global coordination of marketing activities; and ③linkage of marketing activities.

翻译：为了成功地在全球范围内进行竞争，而不仅仅在国内范围进行经营，公司应注意以下几点：①市场经营活动的全球性架构；②市场经营活动的全球性协调；③市场经营活动的联系。

3. Such coordination can be achieved by: ①performing marketing activities using similar method across countries; ②transferring marketing know-how and skills from country to country; ③sequencing marketing programs across countries; ④integrating the efforts of varies marketing groups in different countries.

翻译：这种协调可以通过以下方式获得：①在不同的国家采取相似的方法进行市场营销活动；②把市场营销专门知识和技巧在国家之间传用；③把各国市场营销计划依顺序安排好；④整合各营销团体在不同国家内进行市场营销活动的努力。

4. For example, marketing can unlock economies scale and learning in production and/or R&D by ①supporting the development of universal products by providing the information necessary to develop a physical product design that can be sold worldwide; ②creating demand for more universal products even if historical demand has been for more varied products in different

countries; ③identifying and penetrating segments in many countries to allow the sale of universal products, and ④providing services and/or local accessories that effectively tailor the standard physical product to the local needs.

翻译：例如，市场营销能够通过以下方式达到生产与/或研发的规模经济性与学习经济性：①通过提供必要信息，开发出能够广泛销售的有形产品样式来支持开发全球通用产品；②挖掘对全球通用产品的更大需求，尽管不同国家以往需要的是各式各样的产品；③辨别并深入到各国市场，以便销售全球通用产品；④提供服务和/或当地辅助产品，使标准有形产品有效地与当地需求相适应。

5. Integrated marketing means approaching communications issues from the customer's perspective. Consumers don't separate promotional material or newspaper advertising or community responsiveness into separate compartments. They lump everything together to make judgments about services and organizations.

翻译：综合营销是指从消费者的角度看待沟通的各种问题，在对服务和组织进行评价时，消费者不会把促销材料或报纸广告或公众反馈割裂开去分析，而是看成一个整体。

6. Element of public relations—among them product publicity, special events, spokesman-ship, and similar activities—can enhance a marketing effort. A new discipline—marketing communications—has emerged that uses many of the techniques of public relations.

翻译：公共关系要素——其中包括产品的公众性、特殊性、代表性及其他类似的活动——能促成市场营销。一门新的学科——运用大量公共关系技能的营销沟通学已经形成。

7. Stated another way, although the practice of marketing creates and maintains a market for products and services, and the practice of public relations creates and maintains a hospitable environment in which the organization may operate, marketing success can be nullified by the social and political forces public relations is designed to confront—and thus the interrelationship of the two disciplines.

翻译：换言之，尽管市场营销能为产品和服务创造和维护市场，公共关系的运作能为组织营造和保持一种有利的经验环境，但市场的成功在社会和政治压力下可能会丧失其可能性，而这种压力正是公共关系要面临的挑战。因此，市场营销和公共关系这两门学科的相关性就显而易见了。

8. Although traffic on the world's computer network is booming, most firms that provide the Net's infrastructure — the telecommunications lines and access services— lose money in the business.

翻译：尽管世界计算机网络交通日益繁忙，但多数提供网络基础设施(电信线路及上网服务)的公司在经营中亏损。

9. Another rapidly expanding use of the Net by public relations professionals is the creation

International Marketing and Management 国际营销与管理 Unit 5

and maintenance of Web sites to profile companies, promote produces, or position issues.

翻译：公关行业对网络迅速普及的应用还有另外一个原因，可以创立并维护网站，来描绘公司企业形象，推销产品、定位问题等。

10. The essence of international marketing management is the development of appropriate objective, strategies, and plans that culminate in the successful realization of foreign marketing opportunities. The world marketplace is marked by accelerating change, requiring explicit statements of objectives and strategies.

翻译：国际市场营销管理的实质是制定恰当的最终实现国外市场机遇的目标、战略和计划。以瞬息万变为特征的世界市场需要明确的目标和战略。

11. Although markets overseas are changing and competition increasing, international markets offer attractive opportunities. As a matter of fact, markets across national boundaries frequently offer higher rates of return than domestic markets. However, to make a mark in the international arena, a company needs to define its objectives clearly, choosing appropriate strategies, and develop adequate plans to implement the chosen strategies.

翻译：尽管海外市场变幻莫测，竞争与日俱增，国际市场还是提供了大量诱人的机会。事实上，跨越了国界的市场往往比国内市场提供更高的回报率。不过，想要在国际竞技场取得一席之地，公司需要确定明确的目标，选择恰当的战略，并制订完备的计划来实施这些既定的战略目标。

12. The first role involves facilitating linkage between corporate and subsidiary perspectives. This amounts to providing corporate-wide perspectives relative to its overall mission and direction, both generally and with reference to the subsidiary/country market. The second role includes establishing a worldwide planning system. Such a system is achieved by developing planning procedures and communicating them to subsidiaries. An additional role that corporate headquarters must perform is to serve as a catalyst in creating a planning culture among the subsidiary executives.

翻译：第一个作用是促进总公司与子公司的双方联系，这相当于既要笼统地又要在参考子公司市场或具体国别市场的情况下制定有关公司总体宗旨和方向的全局性思想。第二个作用是建立全球范围内的计划体系，而该计划体系通过确定计划步骤并将这些步骤传达给子公司得以实现。公司总部必须肩负的另一项职责就是充当催化剂，促使在子公司的管理人员中形成一种计划氛围。

13. The majority of successful senior managers do not closely follow the classical rational model of first clarifying goals, assessing the problem, formulating options, estimating likelihoods of success, making a decision, and only then taking action to implement the decision.

翻译：大部分成功的高层管理人员并不拘泥于传统的推理模式，即首先确定目标，然后估定问题，摆出各种可能性，估计成功率，再做决定，最后才付诸行动去实施。

14. Rather, in their day-by-day tactical maneuvers, these senior executives rely on what is vaguely termed intuition to manage a network of interrelated problems that require them to deal with ambiguity, inconsistency, novelty, and surprise, and to integrate action into the process of thinking.

翻译：相反，在这些人的日常决策过程中，他们靠一种定义模糊的直觉应付大量相关问题，这些问题使他们必须在一堆含糊不清、自相矛盾、奇特无比或者令人惊异的事物中做抉择，而且在考虑过程中就要有相应的行动。

15. Given the great uncertainty of many of the management issues that they face, senior managers often instigate a course of action simply to learn more about an issue. They then use the results of the action to develop a more complete understanding of the issue. One implication of thinking/acting cycles is that action is often part of defining the problem, not just of implementing the solution.

翻译：由于管理者们经常面对许多不确定的情况，所以他们鼓励采取各种行动来对问题做一番深入了解。他们藉此对问题做出更深的体会。这种思考行为循环的一个特点即，行动是确定问题的一部分，而不只是解决问题的步骤。

16. Against this gross consumer must be weighed the joint products or services provided by advertising. In the case of electronic advertising, the consumer who views commercial television receives entertainment, while readers of magazines and newspapers receive reduced prices on these publications. The consumer pays directly for some premiums, but also receives nonfood merchandise as an incentive to purchase the product. The "benefits" must, therefore, be subtracted from the gross cost to the consumer to fully assess the net cost of advertising.

翻译：必须将广告提供的联合产品和服务与总消费者相比较。电子广告的消费者收看电视广告，得到了娱乐。同样，报纸、杂志的读者可以以优惠价格购买这些产品。消费者直接为某些赠品付费，但也接受非食物商品来刺激他们购买该产品。因此，这些"利益"必须从消费者的总成本中扣除，以便全面分析广告的净成本。

Part 6　词汇及扩展

national boundaries 国界，国家边界
self-sufficient 自给自足
subsidiaries 下属公司，子公司
domestic 国内的，本土的
barrier 壁垒，障碍

Unit 5

International Marketing and Management 国际营销与管理

crop up 突然出现
stakes 风险
multinationalization 跨国化，跨国公司化
subassembly 组件，部件
linkage 连接，结合
differentiation 差异，区分
sequence 顺序，排序
upstream 上游部门
tailor 使合适……
maxim 格言，箴言
collaboration 合作，协作
credibility 信誉，可信度
proprietor 经营者，所有者，业主
hospitable 热情友好的，舒适的
nullify 使无效，作废，取消
ancillary 副的，从属的
scrutiny 监督，审查
cyberspace 赛博空间
the World Wide Web 万维网
public relations 公共关系
slash 削减
burgeoning 迅速增长的，生机勃勃的
bogged down 停滞，陷入困境
gridlock 僵局，交通堵塞
shovelware 盗版件
customization 用户化，客制化服务
pervasive 普遍的，到处渗透的
Web site 网址，网站
multinational 多国的，跨国公司的，跨国公司
ethnocentrism 民族中心主义
polycentrism 多中心主义
geocentrism 地球中心主义
profit margins 利润率
obsolescence 淘汰

inflation 通货膨胀
scarcity 资源匮乏
Online 在线的，网络的
HTML (Hypertext Markup Language) 超文本标记语言
FAQs (Frequently Asked Questions) 常见问题
merchandising 销售规划，营销
forums 讨论会
connote 意味着，言外之意
antecedents 前因，环境
flawed 有缺陷的，有瑕疵的
amateurish 业余的，不熟练的

Part 7　网络学习资源

　　1．有关客服中心的重要性的讨论可以参考 Erika Rasmussen, *Global Sales on the Line*, *Sales & Marketing Management*, 2000.
　　2．关于沃尔玛的营销策略，可以参看 www.walmartstores.com
　　3．戴尔公司的官方网站：www.dell.com

阅读理解部分参考答案

Unit 2
Passage 1: 1-5　C A A D A

Unit 3
Passage 1: 1-5　C D B C C
Passage 2: 1-4　B D A A
Passage 3: 1-4　B A C A

Unit 4
Passage 1: 1-4　B A D C
Passage 2: 1-5　G B E A C

Unit 5
Passage 1: 1-5　D D C D B
Passage 2: 1-5　D C A B C

参 考 文 献

[1] 李晓娣. 国际经济与贸易专业英语[M]. 哈尔滨：哈尔滨工程大学出版社，2006.
[2] 谢毅斌. 国际经贸英语教程[M]. 北京：中国国际广播出版社，1999.
[3] 冯祥春，孙春立. 国际经贸英语文章精选[M]. 北京：对外经贸大学出版社，2006.
[4] 刘晓玲. 新世纪理工科英语教程[M]. 上海：上海外语教育出版社，2004.
[5] 王湘玲，陶明星，赵瑛. 商务英语阅读(精读本)[M]. 北京：清华大学出版社，2003.
[6] 肖云南. 商务英语选读(泛读本)[M]. 北京：清华大学出版社，2004.
[7] 王洪亮，李浚帆. 新编国际贸易英语教程[M]. 北京：清华大学出版社；北京交通大学出版社，2007.
[8] 刘法公，俞建耀，胡则远. 国际贸易实务英语：解析与阅读提高[M]. 杭州：浙江大学出版社，2006.